Mind the Test

SAT and ACT Grammar Workbook

ISBN: 9798398621143

Dedication

To everyone whose valuable feedback helped this book become a reality.

To my father, whose love of learning was rivaled only by his love for his family. I miss you every day.

To my mother, for instilling in me a passion for education.

And to my husband, for everything.

Thank you for purchasing this book! If you find it useful, please leave an honest review on Amazon.

In addition to 1:1 tutoring, I often lead in-person and virtual group classes about preparing for college, including SAT prep, ACT prep, college admissions essay workshops, study skills, and more. Want to work with me? Contact me at www.mindthetest.com.

Chapter 1. How to Use This Book

Grammar is not often taught directly in schools—at least not in the way presented on the SAT and ACT—so there's a lot to learn. Even though the topics may not be explicitly covered in your school English class, honing these skills for the SAT and ACT will boost your writing and critical reading skills, preparing you for advanced high school and college-level coursework.

> These boxes describe "real-life applications," explaining how the skills in each chapter can help you in high school and college reading and writing assignments.

This book is designed to be read in order, and you should do all the exercises. After working through the book, you should take a timed SAT/ACT—you can find them online or in the official SAT and ACT books, available at the library or any bookstore. Analyze your answers carefully and identify which chapters you need to review, as well as what steps you can take to avoid making the same mistakes in the future; after writing down your ideas and reviewing the chapters, take another practice test. Rinse and repeat.

Here is a **mega-fun quiz** to help you get the most out of the book. You know those quizzes where you answer questions about making a salad and it tells you what kind of magical power you have? Well, this is just like that, except that instead of fun illustrated salad questions, you can choose which made-up test prep student best fits you, and instead of learning your magical power, you learn how to best use this book. You can use your PSAT score or a practice test score to judge.

1. **Score: 700+ SAT Reading/Writing, 31+ ACT English.** Advanced Andrea has done a lot of SAT preparation already, and her practice test scores always come out around 700+ in Evidence-Based Reading and Writing (EBRW), or around 31+ in ACT English, but she's aiming for that perfect score. She feels very confident about the content but sometimes struggles with hard questions and might make what she calls "stupid mistakes."

2. **Score: 600-690 SAT Reading/Writing, 25-30 ACT English.** Middle Matt has taken practice tests and done some studying or tutoring. He feels pretty confident about apostrophes but isn't so sure what the deal is with semicolons.

3. **Score: 590 or lower SAT Reading/Writing, 24 or below ACT English.** Novice Nancy has not done any significant preparation; she may have taken a practice SAT/ACT and read the back cover of a test prep book at the bookstore before gently placing it back on the shelf. She is not sure what is on the test and is not confident in the skills tested.

Does Advanced Andrea speak to your soul? If so, you should examine your practice test results to identify which question types you tend to get wrong or guess on—because guessing right is just one step away from guessing wrong. Then carefully read the corresponding chapters and complete the exercises. If you make any mistakes in the exercises, review the chapter carefully to identify how to avoid that mistake in the future.

As an Advanced Andrea, if you're really pressed for time, you may be able to get away with skipping the reading and going straight to the exercises for the other chapters (but **not** for the chapters that target your weaknesses). You may feel tempted to skip those chapters altogether, but resist the temptation; if you do not learn the underlying rules, your score will plateau and you will be unable to improve it.

Are you a Middle Matt? If so, complete **all** the exercises in the book in order, but you can skim the explanations for any chapters you feel confident with. If you make any mistakes in the exercises, review the chapter carefully to identify how to avoid that mistake in the future. As above, resist the temptation to skip the exercises. Even if you only get one in ten apostrophe questions wrong, it would be a shame to miss that one question on the real test.

Does Nancy Novice sound like you? If so, you're in luck: just read this book cover to cover. Read carefully, complete all brain dumps and study guides, do all the exercises, and check your answers.

A word about "stupid mistakes"

Every test-taker abhors those pesky "stupid mistakes." Based on my years of experience tutoring students all over the world, I don't believe in "stupid mistakes." There is always a way to learn from mistakes, and labeling an error as a "stupid mistake" does nothing to prevent it from happening again. Often, seemingly random "stupid mistakes" actually reveal a pattern, and it usually has to do with a failure to understand the underlying rules. Analyzing wrong answers on exercises and practice tests is essential for improving, so if you find yourself saying, "Oh, it's just a stupid mistake," gently correct yourself and ask instead, "What can I do next time so I don't make that mistake again?"

Chapter 2. Memory, Brain Dumps and Study Guides: Know Your Brain, Own Your Learning

Memorizing vs. learning

Is memorizing the same as learning? Many people would say no. Colloquially, people often think of memorizing as something undesirable, uninteresting, and lacking in practical value. Learning, on the other hand, people think of as more positive, more intellectual, and deeper.

From the perspective of cognitive psychology, however, the two are far more similar than they are different. When we talk about learning, we talk about how the brain forms long-term memories. And when we, conversely, talk about memories, we talk about all kinds of learning, from actions, like learning to tie your shoes or shoot a basketball, to real-life memories that play like a video in your head, like your birthday party last year, to facts, like multiplication tables.

For the sake of this book, think of memorizing as a necessary precursor to learning. In pre-school, you had to learn the ABCs, memorizing the sound that each letter makes. After that, you built on that, learning spelling rules that helped you read and write—like the fact that "write" sounds like "rit," not "wuh-rit-ee." Having memorized that, you kept learning and filing things away into your long-term memory, and you are now able to do advanced tasks like reading this book. Nobody would say that memorizing the ABCs was impractical or antithetical to "true" learning. Memorizing the basics frees up your brain to focus on more advanced things. For this reason, your studying needs to focus on creating long-term memories. Or, as I like to call it, "learning."

This workbook has been designed around how the brain learns best, as proven by decades of cognitive science research done by people much more famous than you or I. There are three principles that have informed this book's structure: active recall, spaced repetition, and interleaving. Rather than just building these features in and leaving it at that, I want to explain to you *why* they work, so that you can do some metacognition—thinking about thinking—and use these in future learning endeavors. As you study, think about how you can use these three principles to make them work for you. Your learning belongs to you; this book is merely a tool to help you meet your goals, both on the SAT/ACT and beyond.

Desirable difficulty

All three principles rely on something called *desirable difficulty*. Desirable difficulty is the idea that people learn best when their brains are working hard. Think of learning like working out to build muscle: If you go to the gym and lift light weights that pose no challenge, you will not get much stronger. In this case, there is not enough desirable difficulty. And if you try to bench-press twice your body weight and drop the weights on yourself and end up in the hospital, that certainly won't help; that difficulty sounds rather undesirable. It's just too hard; you can't do it—yet. With training, that challenge may become the right difficulty level. But if you go to the gym and lift enough weight that it is challenging, but not impossible, you can build muscle.

The same is true of learning. Remembering, or retrieving, information is the "exercise," and the "muscles" you're building are the long-term memories of those facts. The more times you retrieve information, the stronger the long-term memory becomes—if you "exercise" your memories right, using desirable difficulty. If you simply reread your notes, you may feel like you're studying, but it's functionally a lot like lifting those light weights: your brain is not working hard enough at remembering the facts. You may feel like you're learning your notes very well, but this is a **fluency illusion**: reading your notes may be easy now, but a couple days from now, your memory of those notes may be weak because your brain was not challenged by your study sessions. On the other hand, if you just take full-length practice tests over and over, without studying the material enough in between, you are being too hard on your brain; the questions are too difficult, and you won't learn from them—at least, not until you practice with a lot of desirable difficulty.

How can you ensure you are studying with desirable difficulty? I'm glad you asked.

Active recall

Active recall, also known as self-testing, is the single best thing you can do to improve your learning. It occurs when you actively remember information instead of passively reading it. When your brain works hard to retrieve a fact, it helps form a long-term memory. Taking a quiz or filling in a _____ uses active recall.

Ha! Did you catch that? Filling in a blank uses active recall. This makes you stop and think in order to fill in the blank, and your brain has to work that much harder.

Active recall study tool 1: Brain dumps

At the end of each chapter, you will find a brain dump and a study guide. The brain dump looks like this:

BRAIN DUMP!

Write down as much as you can remember from this chapter. DO THIS FROM MEMORY: DO NOT LOOK AT THE BOOK OR YOUR NOTES. You may want to set a timer for five or ten minutes and write continuously.

It is very important to actually write this down, ideally in a physical notebook dedicated to SAT/ACT notes.

The brain dump has two purposes. Firstly, it forces you to use active recall on a myriad of facts. Each time you use active recall on a fact, that memory gets stronger, so doing it for five, ten, or even twenty facts at a time is a highly efficient study method. Secondly, a good brain dump provides you with a nice summary of what you learned.

A brain dump for this chapter so far might look like this:

- Active recall is self-testing. It's gr8 4 memory. Makes memory strong

- Brain dump uses active recall. Writing down everything u remember. Also summary

- ~~Desire??~~ *Desirable* Difficulty = learning should b hard, makes better memories. Like exercise.

- Memorizing important part of learning. Memorize stuff to do harder stuff later, like mem. alphabet to learn to read later.

As you can see, a brain dump need not be in order—active recall was the last topic in the chapter (so far), not the first, but that's OK. Shorthand is fine, and you need not use full sentences, as long as your ideas are clear. Finally, notice that "desire" is crossed out and "desirable" written in. After you finish your brain dump, it's a good idea to double-check what you wrote and fix any mistakes. Mistakes or omissions can be a useful red flag that you need to review that information.

Active recall study tool 2: Study guides

The study guide at the end of each chapter looks like this:

CHAPTER STUDY GUIDE!

After completing the whole chapter, open up your notebook and write ten fill-in-the-blank or short response questions based on your notes. Unlike brain dumps, this does not need to be from memory; feel free to refer back to the book. Include an answer key on the next page so you can quiz yourself in the future.

There are a couple of ways to approach study guides. The first, and most foolproof, way is to simply rewrite your notes with blanks. For example, maybe you took a note like this:

For transition word questions, always underline key terms.

You could rewrite that in your study guide like this:

For _____ word questions, _____ underline key terms.

The answer key would simply say:

Transition, always.

If you want to get a little more creative, you can also rephrase your notes and leave things more open-ended. This can be a little trickier, as you need to make sure your questions are detailed enough that you will be able to answer them a week or month from writing them. However, if you're up for the challenge, this is even better than a simple fill-in-the-blank because the harder your brain works to answer the questions and put the answers into your own words, the more you learn.

Using the high desirable difficulty study guide technique, that same question could be phrased like this:

What should you underline for transition word questions?

The answer key might say:

Underline key terms.

Nothing says you can't use a mix of the two, with some fill-in-the-blanks (like the first example) and some short-answers (like the second example).

When you go through your study guide later, don't write the answers in—use a separate sheet of paper, then check them all at the end. That way, you can use the study guide to test yourself multiple times and use active recall.

Spaced repetition and interleaving

Spaced repetition means spacing out your studying and reviewing at regular intervals. Instead of just reading a chapter and being done with it, it is much more effective to regularly review the material and test yourself on it. For this reason, most chapters will end with a practice test that includes questions covering each topic covered up to that point. The first test will only have two question types, then the next test will have more, and it will build and build until the last test includes every question type. That way, you will be regularly reviewing and your brain won't have time to forget what you have learned.

I like to think of interleaving as "interweaving": mixing different question types together. The real test will not tell you "Hey! This is a subject-verb agreement question!" You will have to figure that out on your own. Interleaving is a highly effective way of helping your brain recognize small but important differences—noticing the difference between a clause question and a modifier question. For this reason, the Interleaving Practice Tests will have different question types all mixed together, so you will have to identify what kind of question it is and how to solve it. Interleaving makes it more difficult at first, but far easier in the long-term, and it has two major benefits. First, it helps your brain learn and remember the techniques. Second, it will help you on the real SAT/ACT, which will, of course, be "interleaved."

Caveat (This is Latin for "beware!"): Since interleaving—mixing up different kinds of questions—is so helpful for learning, why not just do full practice tests from the beginning? Why build it up slowly, with just two types of questions, then three, etc.?

The answer comes down to desirable difficulty. If you have not yet learned how to solve a question, that's not desirable difficulty—that's impossible and a waste of time. Sure, you might guess right, but then you might guess wrong on the real test. Building up your skill set through active recall, spaced repetition, and interleaved practice is the best way to master the SAT, ACT, and any other test.

BRAIN DUMP!

Write down as much as you can remember from this chapter. DO THIS FROM MEMORY: DO NOT LOOK AT THE BOOK OR YOUR NOTES. You may want to set a timer for five or ten minutes and write continuously.

MEMORY, BRAIN DUMPS, AND STUDY GUIDES MINI STUDY GUIDE!

Write 5 questions in your notebook for this mini study guide.

1.   (Sample question: What is a brain dump?)

STUDY GUIDE ANSWER KEY

Write the answer key on the next page.

Chapter 3. Approaching the Writing/English Test and Identifying Type of Question

When doing the test, I strongly recommend reading everything and doing questions as you come to them, and don't forget to read the title of the passage! This is important because many questions rely on context, including the previous and following sentence, as well as the overall main idea of the paragraph, so it is rather important to read the whole paragraph, and not just skip around to the underlined parts. You don't need to focus on the non-underlined parts, but read through them quickly until you hit a question. Then stop, do the question, and continue.

One of the most important skills on the Writing test is identifying what type of question you are dealing with. The best method is glancing at the answer choices and identifying what is changing. Here's an example. What kind of question is this?

I heard the shouts' and saw the girls running away.

A) NO CHANGE

B) the shouts and saw the girls'

C) the shouts' and saw the girl's

D) the shouts and saw the girls

Each answer choice uses the same words; the only thing changing is the use of apostrophes. Thus, this is an apostrophe question. That means you don't need to worry about all those comma rules, the main idea of the paragraph, or anything other than apostrophe rules. By glancing down the answer choices to see what is changing, you can make sure you are focusing on the right thing. (The correct answer is D, by the way, as nothing is possessive. If you're not sure why, check out the chapter on apostrophes.)

Let's try a harder one:

We saw that the myriad paintings of the highly decorated admiral were on the wall.

A) NO CHANGE

B) was on the wall.

C) are on the wall.

D) is on the wall.

What's changing? The wording is largely the same, so it isn't a question of word choice or overhauling the sentence. The only difference is in verb tense (were/are, was/is) and number (were/was, are/is). This is a classic example of a combined subject-verb agreement and verb tense question. Now that we know what kind of question it is, we know how to solve it. (The answer is A because the subject is "paintings" and the sentence is in the past, based on the other verb, "saw." See the subject-verb agreement chapter to learn more.)

If we had not taken a split second to glance at the answer choices and identify the type of question, we might have spent far more time focusing on the wrong thing, wasting time and decreasing accuracy. It's worth it to take a quick look at the answers.

BRAIN DUMP!

Write down as much as you can remember from this chapter. DO THIS FROM MEMORY: DO NOT LOOK AT THE BOOK OR YOUR NOTES. You may want to set a timer for five or ten minutes and write continuously.

APPROACHING THE WRITING/ENGLISH TEST MINI STUDY GUIDE!

Write 5 questions in your notebook for this mini study guide.

1. (Sample question: How can the answer choices help you understand what a question is asking?)

STUDY GUIDE ANSWER KEY

Write the answer key on the next page.

Chapter 4: What Is Grammar?

What is grammar? Nouns. Commas. Clauses. Apostrophes. Red marks on assignments. You know: grammar. There are only two types of grammar: correct and incorrect. That's what you've always been told. It has to be right. Right?

Wrong.

Let's try that again.

Let's consider grammar from the linguist's perspective. A linguist is someone who studies all kinds of languages and tries to understand the differences and similarities. A linguist is *not* someone who thinks their way of speaking or writing is *better* than anyone else's. With that in mind, let's ask our question again:

What is grammar?

Grammar is the system that a language uses to create meaning and words in order. Yes, grammar does include things like nouns, commas, clauses, and apostrophes, but most things that are called "incorrect grammar" are not actually incorrect—they're just based on different grammar rules.

Here is an English sentence with incorrect grammar:

Eat to potato baked love me sour cream with sister.

Huh?

Let's fix it, using Standard Academic American English—the kind of English grammar you use in school and on the SAT/ACT:

My sister loves to eat baked potatoes with sour cream.

What was wrong with the "incorrect" version? Gosh, what *wasn't* wrong with it? Well, most of the words were correct, but there were some errors; for example, instead of "my" it said "me." The biggest problem was the word order. It just didn't make any sense. Do you know anyone who talks like that? Probably not. From a linguist's point of view, the only "incorrect" grammar is something like that sentence: something that nobody would ever say because it just doesn't make sense.

Dialects: flavors of language

The confusion is because there are many different dialects, or types, of English. I like to think of each dialect as a separate flavor of language. Just as ice cream may be chocolate, vanilla, strawberry, or mint-chocolate-chip-rocky-road-fudgesicle, and no one flavor is the "real" or "correct" ice cream flavor, there are many flavors of language, and no one is the real or correct version. For example, people in England speak and write slightly differently from people in the US, which can be a little confusing when someone in America reads a book written in the UK. Even within the US, there are a few different dialects, often spoken in different regions or communities.

Many people never realize that they speak a different dialect, instead erroneously thinking that they are just really bad at grammar. This is not true. You are not bad at grammar; you are good at a different kind of grammar. All you need to do is practice learning the rules of Standard Academic American English grammar, the kind needed on the SAT and in college, and you'll get good at that kind, too.

Here are some examples of sentences in different dialects of English that are often mistaken (even by English teachers!) as "incorrect" grammar, but are actually *not* incorrect—they're just a different dialect:

1. My sister **love** to eat baked potatoes with sour cream. (Some dialects have different grammar rules for subject-verb agreement.)

2. The squirrel enjoyed eating nuts, **fruit and** french fries. (Some dialects have different grammar rules for commas.)

3. My **favourite flavour** of ice cream is chocolate, **whilst** my sister's **favourite** is vanilla. (Some dialects have different spelling and vocabulary rules.)

The SAT/ACT has a stricter definition of "correct" grammar because it is only looking for one particular dialect: Standard Academic American English.

Here is how we would write those sentences in Standard:

1. My sister **loves** to eat baked potatoes with sour cream. (Standard adds an "s" after a present tense verb.)

2. The squirrel enjoyed eating nuts, **fruit, and** french fries. (Standard adds a comma before the "and" in a list.)

3. My **favorite flavor** of ice cream is chocolate, **while** my sister's **favorite** is vanilla. (Standard uses different spellings.)

Many people mistakenly think that Standard is the only "right" way of speaking, but as you have seen, that's not quite true. Would you tell a University of Cambridge English professor that her writing is "wrong" because she writes using British comma rules? Probably not. So if someone says that it's "bad grammar" to say "My sister love baked potatoes," they're wrong; it's like saying that strawberry ice cream is bad chocolate ice cream, when really, it's just a different kind of ice cream. The Cambridge professor and the sibling of the potato-lover aren't using *bad* grammar, but they're using *different* grammar from the Standard that the test requires; to do well on the test, they will have to study the rules of Standard Academic American English.

All that is to say this: If some of the grammar rules in this book seem strange, confusing, or just plain different from how you usually talk, that's OK—just treat SAT/ACT grammar as a semi-separate entity from real-life grammar. In fact, many professional authors violate some of the grammar rules you will read about in this section. (Even some of the passages on the Reading section of the SAT/ACT will violate some of the rules!) **So don't worry too much**

about what is "right" and "wrong" grammar; just focus on learning the Standard grammar the SAT and ACT want you to know.

BRAIN DUMP!

Write down as much as you can remember from this chapter. DO THIS FROM MEMORY: DO NOT LOOK AT THE BOOK OR YOUR NOTES. You may want to set a timer for five or ten minutes and write continuously.

WHAT IS GRAMMAR? MINI STUDY GUIDE!

Write 5 questions in your notebook for this mini study guide.

STUDY GUIDE ANSWER KEY

Write the answer key on the next page.

Chapter 5: Parts of Speech: Nouns & Pronouns

Nouns

A noun is a person, place, thing, or concept. Nouns can be **singular**, meaning there's only one, or **plural**, meaning there are two or more.

Here are some singular nouns: chair, computer, cat, mother, judgment, idea.

Here are some plural nouns: chairs, computers, cats, mothers, judgments, ideas.

Got it? Good.

EXERCISE 1

Underline the nouns. Each sentence may have more than one.

1. Where is the remote?

2. Mom, please close the window!

3. The butter is in the refrigerator.

4. Last week, there was an interesting article in the newspaper.

5. In recent years, people have enjoyed looking at photographs of adorable dogs on the internet.

ANSWER KEY

1. Remote

2. Mom, window

3. Butter, refrigerator

4. Week, article, newspaper

5. Years, people, photographs, dogs, internet

What is the subject?

The **subject** of a sentence is the main actor in the sentence. Ask "Who/what is acting?" or "Who/what is doing the verb?" and you'll find the subject. **Every sentence needs a subject.**

Here are some examples of sentences with the subject in **bold**.

1. **The girl** eats a sandwich.
2. **Bob** forgot to clear the table.
3. After sleeping through my alarm, **I** missed the bus.
4. Yesterday, **those letters** arrived in the mail.

As you can see, the subject often, but not always, comes at or near the beginning of the sentence.

We'll discuss subjects in greater detail later on, when we discuss something called **subject-verb agreement**.

Noun agreement: singular or plural?

Hot tip: If one answer choice has a singular noun while another answer choice has the same noun but plural, read the sentences around it to identify whether it should be singular or plural.

Here's an example:

Both my brother and my sister want <u>to be a video game designer</u> when they grow up.

A) NO CHANGE

B) to become a designer of video games

C) to be video game designers

D) video game designing

First, let's identify which type of question this is *not*. Doing a quick scan down the answer choices, we can see that the wording is similar in all of them, so it is not a vocabulary question. There are no punctuation differences, so this is not a punctuation question.

What type of question *is* it? Notice that options A and C are exactly the same, except that A uses the singular "a video game designer" and C uses the plural "video game designers." Which is correct?

To find out, inspect the context. Earlier, it says "both my brother and my sister," which is plural. Option A, which may "sound right" to many people, is there to trick you: because it says "designer" in the singular, it refers to only one person. Do my brother and sister dream of one day fusing together into one giant video game designing person, like some kind of giant monster? Probably not. They probably want to grow up to be two separate people who are both video game designers, so we need a plural noun. C is the answer.

EXERCISE 2

1. As a reward for our good grades, my mom gave my sister and me <u>an ice cream cone</u>.

   A) NO CHANGE

   B) ice cream cones

   C) ice cream in a cone

   D) cones being full of ice cream

2. All the students wracked <u>they're brain</u> to try to think of the solution.

   A) NO CHANGE

   B) its brain

   C) their brains

   D) their brain

3. Moths come out of cocoons, while butterflies <u>come out of a chrysalis</u>.

    A) NO CHANGE

    B) having come out of a chrysalis

    C) come out of the chrysalis

    D) come out of chrysalises

ANSWER KEY

1. B. Since answers A and B are the same except for the "s" in "cones," this is a singular/plural noun question. Did my mom give us just one ice cream cone to split, or did we each get a separate cone? Most likely, we each got our own cone, so there were two cones. B is the best and shortest plural answer. D is also plural, but it is too wordy; "being" is also a red flag word: "being" is rarely correct.

2. C. How many brains do all the students have: just one giant brain that they share? Probably not. They all have their own brains, so we need a plural. C is the only plural. (D is a trick answer: it seemingly fixes the pronoun error, but it does not give us the plural "brains" that we need.)

3. D. Since answers A and D are the same except for the singular/plural number of the last word, this is a singular/plural noun question. Do all butterflies come out of one giant chrysalis? No, they each have their own. Thus, we need a plural, and only D provides that. Notice also that this sentence compares two things: moths and cocoons, and butterflies and _____. Since "cocoons" is plural, it makes sense for "chrysalises" to match that and be plural, too.

Pronouns

A pronoun is a nonspecific word that stands in for a noun.

Here are some pronouns: he, him, she, her, it, they, them, we, us, one.

On the SAT, every pronoun must have a stated **antecedent** before it. The antecedent is the word the pronoun is referring to. Here's an example:

My **brother** is tall, and **he** loves playing sports.

"He" is the pronoun. "Brother" is the antecedent.

EXERCISE 3

Star the pronoun. Underline the antecedent.

1. Sarah is short, but she is great at basketball.

2. Although the book was written a century ago, it is still relevant today.

3. When my grandfather tells a story, he never knows when to stop talking.

4. The article about sharks was influential; it changed people's minds about the animals.

5. My favorite movie is fairly obscure; most people haven't heard of it.

ANSWER KEY

1. Pronoun: she. Antecedent: Sarah

2. Pronoun: it. Antecedent: book (or the book)

3. Pronoun: he. Antecedent: grandfather (or my grandfather)

4. Pronoun: it. Antecedent: article (or the article. NOT sharks)

5. Pronoun: it. Antecedent: movie (or my favorite movie)

Hot tip: If some answer choices say "it" and some say "they," find the antecedent and identify whether it is singular or plural. Cross out the answer choices that don't match.

EXERCISE 4

1. My friend loves that song, but I don't like <u>it</u> that much.

    A) NO CHANGE

    B) its

    C) them

    D) these

2. Most scientists find the results to be convincing, but not all are convinced of <u>it's</u> accuracy.

    A) NO CHANGE

    B) Its

    C) their

    D) they're

3. The origin of the stars has been debated for millenia, and people still debate about <u>them</u> today.

    A) NO CHANGE

B) those

C) its

D) it

4. Although the collection of poems was long, I enjoyed reading <u>it</u>.

    A) NO CHANGE

    B) some of those items

    C) them

    D) theirs

5. Although the president tried to be patient with the committee, he began to grow frustrated with <u>them</u>.

    A) NO CHANGE

    B) those of them

    C) it

    D) It's

6. The lion is my favorite animal. <u>Their</u> graceful and beautiful.

    A) NO CHANGE

    B) They're

    C) Its

    D) It's

ANSWER KEY

1. A. Since the answer choices include various versions of "it" and "they," ask what the antecedent is—that is, what don't I like? I don't like that song. How many songs is it? Just one, so it's singular. Thus, we need some form of "it." A is the simplest and best answer. If you are not sure about A vs. B, read the chapter on apostrophes for help.

2. C. Since the answer choices include various versions of "it" and "they," ask what the antecedent is—that is, not all are convinced of what's accuracy? Not all are convinced of the accuracy of the results, so "results" is the antecedent, and it's plural. Thus, either C or D is needed. D would be short for "they are," so the answer is C. If you are not sure about C vs. D, read the chapter on apostrophes for help.

3. D. Since the answer choices include various versions of "it" and "they" (or them), ask what the antecedent is—that is, what do people still debate today? People debate the origin of the stars. Is it singular or plural? Well, how many origins are we talking about? Just one—otherwise, we would say "origins" instead of "origin." Thus, the antecedent is singular and we need some form of "it," not "they." D is correct. If you are not sure about C vs. D, read the chapter on apostrophes for help.

4. A. Since the answer choices include various versions of "it" and "they" (or them), ask what the antecedent is—that is, what did I enjoy reading? I enjoyed reading the collection of poems. How many collections is it? Just one collection, so it's singular. Even though it is made up of many poems, it is just one collection, so it is singular. The only singular answer choice is A.

5. C. Since the answer choices include various versions of "it" and "they" (or them), ask what the antecedent is—that is, who was he frustrated with? He was frustrated with the committee. It's just one committee (otherwise, we would say "committees"). Even though the committee is made up of multiple people, it's just one committee, so it is singular. Thus, we need a singular word like "it."

6. D. Since the answer choices include various versions of "it" and "they," ask what the antecedent is—that is, what is graceful and beautiful? "The lion" is singular, so even though it sounds strange to many, "it" is the matching pronoun. We need "it is," so D works. If you are not sure about C vs. D, read the chapter on apostrophes for help.

Hot tip: Every pronoun must have an unambiguous antecedent. If three answer choices are pronouns and one is an actual noun, the noun is probably correct.

Let's try this one together:

The doctor and her daughter were both tall, but <u>she</u> had lighter hair.

A) NO CHANGE

B) the doctor

C) it

D) that

The first thing to notice is that all the answer choices except for B are some kind of pronoun or pronoun-like "th"-word. Based on that alone, B is probably the answer.

However, let's dig deeper. This is a red flag that we need more details about the pronoun, so ask, "Who is "she" referring to? Who had lighter hair?" It could be the doctor, or it could be her daughter. It is ambiguous. Only option B explains who precisely had lighter hair, so B is the answer.

Hot tip: On the SAT/ACT, shorter is usually better, but that is only if the shortest answer does not delete anything important. In this case, the shortest answers leave out important information about who the antecedent is, so the (slightly) longer answer is correct.

EXERCISE 5

1. The waiter was carrying a cup of hot coffee and a jug of lemonade, and he spilled _it_ all over himself.

    A) NO CHANGE

    B) this

    C) the beverage

    D) the lemonade

2. First, the count advised the king. Next, the duke advised the king. The king considered and ultimately decided to do what _he_ had suggested.

    A) NO CHANGE

    B) that one

    C) the count

    D) one

3. _It_ has been hot and humid.

    A) NO CHANGE

    B) The weather

    C) They

    D) That

A) D. What did he spill? The coffee or the lemonade? The antecedent of "it" is unclear in every answer choice other than D.

B) C. The king did what who suggested? The count or the duke? The antecedent of "he" is unclear in every answer other than C.

C) B. Although this may sound OK colloquially, the SAT would say that option A, "it," has no stated antecedent, and thus is incorrect. B is the only option that states an antecedent.

BRAIN DUMP!

Write down as much as you can remember from this chapter. DO THIS FROM MEMORY: DO NOT LOOK AT THE BOOK OR YOUR NOTES. You may want to set a timer for five or ten minutes and write continuously.

NOUNS & PRONOUNS STUDY GUIDE!

Write 10 questions in your notebook for this study guide.

STUDY GUIDE ANSWER KEY

Write the answer key on the next page.

Chapter 6: Parts of Speech: Verbs

Verbs are action words. Run, walk, sit, stand, fight, hug, laugh, cry…

On the SAT and ACT, though, verbs are so much more.

Here are the **most important fundamental verb facts:**

1. "Is," "are," "was," "were," and all the other tenses of "to be" are real verbs. Often, "is" is the main verb in a sentence.

2. In general, verbs stick to the same **tense** as the verbs in the sentences around them. For example, we would say, "There **was** a fascinating discovery last week when researchers **found** a hidden tomb." Both "was" and "found" are in the **past tense**.

3. "ing" words (i.e. walking, running) are never main verbs by themselves. For example, in "She is walking," the main verb is "is." We can also say that the full verb phrase is "is walking." We can **not** say that the main verb is just "walking."

Take a deep breath. That was a lot of verb facts.

Are you ready for the fourth, final, and my personal favorite verb fact?

4. "Ing" words are often **gerunds. Gerunds act like singular nouns**.

Gerunds act like singular nouns? What does that mean? I'm glad you asked!

What part of speech is the underlined word?

>   Soccer is fun.

If you guessed "noun," you're correct! Try these ones:

>   Basketball is exciting.

Pizza is good.

Cabbage is gross.

Noun, noun, noun. These are all nouns. This is probably not exciting yet.

But wait! What about this one?

Running is fun.

"Running" is a gerund, and it seems to be replacing "soccer" in the sentence. Well, if "soccer" is a noun, and "running" is replacing it, is "running" a noun? Hmm. Let's try the other sentences:

Reading is exciting.

Sleeping is good.

Picking your nose is gross.

In every case, we simply replaced the noun subject with a gerund (or gerund phrase, in the last example). It may not exactly be a noun, but it sure acts like one.

How can we tell that it's acting like a singular noun? You tell me. What's wrong with this sentence?

X Running are fun.

We haven't learned about subject-verb agreement yet, so I'll just say that it's wrong because the subject doesn't match the verb. What about this one?

X Baking cookies are fun.

Again, the subject is the gerund "baking," and gerunds are singular. It should say this:

Baking cookies is fun.

Subject-Verb Agreement: Singular/plural, but for verbs!

What is subject-verb agreement? To answer that, we must first talk about subjects and clauses.

We won't go too deeply into the grammar rules of clauses and sentences yet. Suffice to say that **the subject of a sentence is the main actor: the person or thing that is doing the verb. I** like to think of it as **"who or what is verbing."**

Here's an example:

The girl eats the cake.

First, let's label the sentence with parts of speech:

	NOUN	VERB		NOUN
The	girl	eats	the	cake.

The verb is "eats." Who or what is eating? The girl is eating. Thus, the girl is the subject.

Let's add that to our labeling:

	SUBJECT			
	NOUN	VERB		NOUN
The	girl	eats	the	cake.

Got it? Good.

In Standard Academic American English—the dialect used on the SAT/ACT and in school—there are strict rules for whether or not a verb has an "s" at the end in the present tense. Some students find it easy to tell what "sounds right," while other students find it difficult; however, the SAT/ACT uses this intuitive sense of "sounding right" against you by using tricky sentences, so it is worth reading through this list regardless of your linguistic background.

Pay special attention to the he/she/it row:

Singular	Plural
I eat	We eat
You eat	You eat
He/she/it eat**s**	They eat

Notice that the present tense singular adds an "s" (eat**s**), while the plural does not (eat).

Here is the same sort of chart, but for "to be" verbs in the present tense:

Singular	Plural

I am	We are
You are	You are
He/she/it **is**	They are

And for "to be" verbs in the past tense:

Singular	Plural
I was	We were
You were	You were
He/she/it wa**s**	They were

Notice that even though this looks somewhat different, "is" still ends in "s."

This brings me to one of my favorite tips to help remember the chart. I call it **The S Rule**:

A <u>S</u>ingular <u>S</u>ubject takes a verb that ends in "<u>s</u>."

If you read The S Rules out loud, pretend you are a snake and really "ssssss" it. It helps you remember. Really.

Hot tip: The two keys to subject-verb agreement are identifying the correct subject and making sure the verb has the right ending.

Would you like to hear my other favorite subject-verb agreement trick? Of course you would! It's called **Substitution.**

Substitution

Substitution, or "subject substitution," is a technique aimed at those students who have an intuitive sense of what "sounds right" for subject-verb agreement in Standard Academic American English. That might mean you if you find it easy to spot the error here:

The children is playing outside.

If you automatically thought, "It sounds better to say 'are' instead of 'is,'" substitution will be a particularly useful tool for you.

The SAT intentionally takes advantage of this intuitive sense of "sounding right" and uses it against you by giving you tricky sentences with confusing subjects. Try this one:

The venerated council, consisting of highly decorated military officials and politicians,

<u>have</u> decided to act.

A) NO CHANGE

B) has

C) are

D) is

Does it sound right or wrong? Intuition breaks down at this point. It might sound somewhat OK, but it lacks the clear sense of "Yes, that's correct" or "No, that's wrong" that easier, shorter sentences have. In fact, if you use only your intuition on subject-verb agreement questions, you will frequently guess wrong.

To solve this, we must find the subject. We must ask, "Who or what is verbing?" That is, who or what decided to act? The council decided to act, so the council is the subject.

Should it be singular or plural? Well, how many councils is it? Just one council, so it is singular.

OK, great. We found our subject. We identified that it is singular. Now what?

There are two ways to move forward.

1. If you remember the chart or the S Rule, you should remember that a singular subject needs a verb ending with an "s" (in the present tense), so the answer must be B or D. Only B provides the correct way to form the present perfect tense—or "sounds right"—so B is the answer.

2. Use **substitution**. How? Why, I am glad you asked!

Substitution means plugging in a singular or plural pronoun instead of a singular or plural subject. **You can use "it" instead of a singular subject, and you can use "they" instead of a plural subject.** This lets you more easily decide which verb sounds better.

Let's try it with the example above:

The venerated council, consisting of highly decorated military officials and politicians,

>   have decided to act.

A) NO CHANGE

B) has

C) are

D) is

We already decided that the subject is "council," which is singular, and perhaps we can identify that it should be A or B based on context. But should it say "the council has" or "the council have"?

Let's use substitution. Instead of "the council," we can use "it." Now the sentence says this:

>   (A) It have decided to act.

>   (B) It has decided to act.

If you are someone with an intuitive sense of "what sounds right," then B clearly sounds more right than A. If not, use the S Rule instead. Either will help you find out that B is the right answer.

Active vs. Passive Voice

Remember that in general, shorter is better. With that in mind, which sentence do you think is best?

    A) The cake was eaten by the girl.
    B) The girl ate the cake.

B is shorter, so B is better.

In addition, B uses the **active voice**, while A uses the **passive voice**. Try to figure out the difference between the active and passive voice by examining these examples; notice that there are two passive options, both grammatically correct. Pay close attention to what happens to the subject and the verb:

Active	Passive
My dog ate his food.	The food was eaten by my dog. The food was eaten.
The teacher reads the poem.	The poem is read by the teacher. The poem is read.
He cooked dinner.	Dinner was cooked by him. Dinner was cooked.

Try to guess the rules by circling the correct word.

    1. An active sentence generally has the subject **before/after** the verb.
    2. A(n) **active/passive** sentence may completely leave out who is doing the verb.
    3. A(n) **active/passive** sentence has "is" or "was" before the verb.
    4. A(n) **active/passive** sentence often leaves the subject until the end, after "by."

Ready for the answers?

    1. An active sentence generally has the subject **before** the verb.
    2. A **passive** sentence may completely leave out who is doing the verb.
    3. A **passive** sentence has "is" or "was" before the verb.
    4. A **passive** sentence often leaves the subject until the end, after "by."

BRAIN DUMP!

Write down as much as you can remember from this chapter. DO THIS FROM MEMORY: DO NOT LOOK AT THE BOOK OR YOUR NOTES. You may want to set a timer for five or ten minutes and write continuously.

EXERCISE 1

1. The S Rule says that a _____ subject matches with a verb that ends in _____.

2. Substitution means you can use "it" instead of a _____ subject and _____ instead of a plural subject.

3. Substitution is useful for some students because it helps them figure out _____.

4. True/False: You should **not** "trust your gut" with singular/plural on the SAT and ACT because the tests will use it to trick you.

5. True/False: Active sentences are usually shorter than passive sentences, so active is better.

6. Which sentence is better and why?

    A) Joey plays the guitar.
    B) The guitar is played by Joey.

7. Which sentence is better and why?

    A) I read a fascinating book last week.
    B) A fascinating book was read by me last week.

8. Which sentence is better and why?

    A) Mr. Mason boiled the potatoes.
    B) The potatoes were boiled.

9. Which sentence is better and why?

    A) The car is being washed by my brother.
    B) My brother is washing the car.

10. Which sentence is better and why?

    A) Last week, a new planet was discovered.
    B) Last week, scientists discovered a new planet.

EXERCISE 2

Sentence mapping: Circle (or **bold**) all nouns. <u>Underline</u> all verbs.

1. The horse whinnied nervously.

2. John spent all morning looking for his keys.

3. Sam laughed because she had hidden John's keys very effectively.

4. Summer is the hottest season.

5. My guinea pigs are always squeaking loudly.

EXERCISE 3

1. I like watching TV, but going out to the movies <u>are</u> even more fun.

    A) NO CHANGE

    B) is

    C) was

    D) were

2. Knitting sweaters <u>is</u> my hobby; I try to knit a little bit every day.

    A) NO CHANGE

    B) was

    C) being

    D) are

3. The researcher reported that determining the validity of the results <u>were</u> difficult.

    A) NO CHANGE

B) are

C) was

D) have been

4. The artist's lifestyle of constantly creating paintings <u>are</u> not as easy as it sounds.

   A) NO CHANGE

   B) is

   C) were

   D) have not been

CHAPTER 6 ANSWER KEY

EXERCISE 1

1. The S Rule says that a **sssingular** subject matches with a verb that ends in **s.**

2. Substitution means you can use "it" instead of a **singular** subject and **they** instead of a plural subject.

3. Substitution is useful for some students because it helps them figure out **what sounds right**.

4. **True. Don't trust your gut**

5. True.

6. A. Sentence A is shorter and active, so it is better. Sentence B is longer and passive. "Is ___ed by" is a red flag that it is passive.

7. A. Sentence A is shorter and active, so it is better. Sentence B is longer and passive. "Was ___ by" is a red flag that it is passive.

8. A. Sentence A is active, so it is better (even though it is not shorter in this case). B is passive because it cuts out the person doing the action and says "were ___ed."

9. B. Sentence B is active, so it is better. It contains the subject, stating who is washing the car.

10. B. Sentence B is active, so it is better. It contains the subject, stating who discovered the planet.

EXERCISE 2

1. Nouns: horse. Verbs: whinnied

2. Nouns: John; morning; keys. Verbs: spent (NOT looking)

3. Nouns: Sam; keys (or John's keys. NOT just John). Verbs: laughed; had hidden

4. Nouns: summer; season. Verbs: is

5. Nouns: guinea pigs (or my guinea pigs. NOT just my). Verbs: are (or are squeaking. NOT just squeaking)

EXERCISE 3

1. B. The gerund "going" is the subject, so it is singular and matches with "is." It needs to be present tense because of the other present-tense verb, "like."

2. A. The gerund "knitting" is the subject, so it is singular and matches with "is." It needs to be present tense because of the other present-tense verb, "try."

3. C. What was difficult? Determining was difficult, so the singular "determining" is the subject. The S Rule says that in this situation, a singular subject needs a verb ending in "s," so it must be C. We could also use substitution and plug in "it" instead of "determining." That way, we could turn the sentence into "It...was difficult."

4. B. What is not as easy as it sounds? The lifestyle is not as easy as it sounds. Thus, the subject is the singular "lifestyle." The S Rule says that in this situation, a singular subject needs a verb ending in "s," so it must be B. We could also use substitution and plug in "it" instead of "lifestyle." That way, we could turn the sentence into "It...is not."

VERBS STUDY GUIDE!

Write 10 questions in your notebook for this study guide.

STUDY GUIDE ANSWER KEY

Write the answer key on the next page.

Chapter 7: Prepositions

Prepositions are (usually) little grammar words that tell us details, such as where something is. They come at the beginning of prepositional phrases. Here are some prepositional phrases:

On the fridge

In the drawer

Near the desk

Under your book

Above the box

Of the interesting story

Outside the lines

To my school

By the famous author

From Bob

For you

Notice any patterns?

A prepositional phrase always starts with a preposition and ends with a noun (or pronoun).

Hot tip: Cross out prepositional phrases to find the subject.

Try this example:

The picture of my favorite turtles <u>are</u> on my refrigerator.

A) NO CHANGE

B) were

C) have been

D) is

Since the answer choices vary between singular/plural number and verb tense, let's find the subject. Ask, "What are on my refrigerator?" The picture of my favorite turtles.

But is that singular or plural?

To find out the **real** subject, cross out the prepositional phrase:

The picture ~~of my favorite turtles~~ <u>are</u> on my refrigerator.

The real subject is "the picture," which is singular. The answer is D because "is" is the only singular verb in the answer choices.

BRAIN DUMP!

Write down as much as you can remember from this chapter. DO THIS FROM MEMORY: DO NOT LOOK AT THE BOOK OR YOUR NOTES. You may want to set a timer for five or ten minutes and write continuously.

EXERCISE 1

Circle the prepositions.

1. To, for, him, on, yes, your, my, with

2. Without, at, me, near, house, the, and

3. Above, bought, by, from, about, talk, out

4. Under, down, up, yesterday, before, after

5. Today, across, pet, move, his, above,

6. Cross, being, is, around, behind, about

7. Below, under, unlikely, probably, at, often

8. Beneath, beside, briefly, between, beyond

9. By, for, in, from, inside, into, near, of, off

10. On, to, try, toward, through, under

EXERCISE 2

Cross out the prepositional phrases. (There may be more than one per sentence.)

1. Taylor put the photo of Poppy, her beloved puppy, in a frame.

2. The photo of Poppy took pride of place in the middle of the desk, and the dog liked to bark at it.

3. Anyone can see that Victoria's opinion of birds is immutably positive.

4. Nobody thinks more highly of birds than Victoria.

5. After eating a late dinner at home, Noah sat on the couch to watch whatever was on TV.

EXERCISE 3

Cross out the prepositional phrases. Underline the subject of the **bolded** verb.

1. Snuffie and Winnie, the most fabulous pugs in the world, **ran** around the yard and barked at squirrels.

2. Jeff scratched an itch on his head as he tried to decide how many types of melons **were required** for his party.

3. There **were** already four cantaloupes in his shopping cart, and there were watermelons and honeydews on the shelves at the store, too.

4. Jess woke up in the morning and discovered that a cat **was** asleep on her face.

5. Upon hearing that the human was awake, the cat, previously in repose, **jumped** up and ran across the floor to the food bowl.

CHAPTER 7 ANSWER KEY

EXERCISE 1

1. To, for, on, with

2. Without, at, near

3. Above, by, from, about, out

4. Under, down, up, before, after

5. Across, above

6. Around, behind, about

7. Below, under, at

8. Beneath, beside, between, beyond

9. By, for, in, from, inside, into, near, of, off

10. On, to, toward, through, under

EXERCISE 2

1. Taylor put the photo ~~of Poppy~~, her beloved puppy, ~~in a frame~~.

2. The photo ~~of Poppy~~ took pride ~~of place in the middle of the desk~~, and the dog liked to bark ~~at it~~.

3. Anyone can see that Victoria's opinion ~~of birds~~ is immutably positive.

4. Nobody thinks more highly ~~of birds~~ than Victoria.

5. ~~After eating a late dinner~~ at home, Noah sat ~~on the couch~~ to watch whatever was ~~on TV~~.

EXERCISE 3

1. <u>Snuffie and Winnie</u>, the most fabulous pugs ~~in the world~~, **ran** ~~around the yard~~ and barked ~~at squirrels~~.

2. Jeff scratched an itch ~~on his head~~ as he tried to decide how many <u>types</u> ~~of melons~~ **were required** ~~for his party~~.

3. There **were** already <u>four cantaloupes</u> ~~in his shopping cart~~, and there were watermelons and honeydews ~~on the shelves~~ ~~at the store~~, too.

4. Jess woke up ~~in the morning~~ and discovered that <u>a cat</u> **was** asleep ~~on her face~~.

5. Upon hearing that the human was awake, <u>the cat</u>, previously ~~in repose~~, **jumped** up and ran ~~across the floor~~ ~~to the food bowl~~.

PREPOSITIONS STUDY GUIDE!

Write 10 questions in your notebook for this study guide.

STUDY GUIDE ANSWER KEY

Write the answer key on the next page.

Chapter 8: Crossing Out Comma Phrases

Comma phrases, in which an unimportant idea is surrounded by two commas (like this one), are common on the SAT and ACT. Because they are nonessential, they can always be deleted from the sentence. So, the previous sentence could say, "Comma phrases are common on the SAT and ACT," without the middle part, and it would still make sense.

Here are some more examples:

1. The girl, a basketball player, had little free time.

2. The boat, on the other hand, might sink.

3. My mom, however, was unamused.

> Hot tip: Comma phrases often come between the subject and verb. Cross them out to find the subject.

Let's cross out the comma phrases to find the subjects of these sentences:

1. The girl, ~~a basketball player~~, had little free time. **Subject = the girl**

2. The boat, ~~on the other hand~~, might sink. **Subject = the boat**

3. My mom, ~~however~~, was unamused. **Subject = my mom**

Although a comma phrase often starts after the subject and ends before the verb, comma phrases can come at the beginning or end of a sentence, too.

4. However, my mom was unamused.

5. My mom was unamused, however.

6. On the other hand, the boat might sink.

7. The boat might sink, on the other hand.

(You might notice that technically, there is only one comma in sentences 4-7 because the comma phrase starts/ends the sentence. That's OK; it would be silly to write:

X   ,However, my mom was unamused.

So it's still a normal comma phrase even though there's technically just one comma.)

Hot tip: Read the sentence to make sure you crossed out the right thing.

Don't assume that just because you see two commas, you should cross out whatever comes between them. Consider:

In 1940, the ship, having been out of commission for nearly two decades, was finally

disposed of.

What comma phrases should we cross out or delete here?

Well, you might have noticed that "the ship" has a comma before and after it, so let's see what happens if we cross it out:

In 1940, ~~the ship~~, having been out of commission for nearly two decades, was finally

disposed of.

Uh-oh.

That sentence is missing something important. We must have crossed out the wrong thing. Let's try again:

~~In 1940~~, the ship, ~~having been out of commission for nearly two decades~~, was finally disposed of.

Now our sentence says, "The ship was finally disposed of." That sounds better.

Let's back up. What did we actually cross out?

We crossed out a classic comma phrase, "having been...decades," which came between the subject ("the ship") and the verb ("was").

We also crossed out an **introductory comma phrase**, "In 1940." These are very common, and crossing them out can help make long, complicated sentences easier to deal with.

BRAIN DUMP!

Write down as much as you can remember from this chapter. DO THIS FROM MEMORY: DO NOT LOOK AT THE BOOK OR YOUR NOTES. You may want to set a timer for five or ten minutes and write continuously.

EXERCISE 1

Cross out all nonessential comma phrases to make these sentences simpler.

Hint: Look for introductory comma phrases at the beginning, as well as comma phrases in the middle *and* end of the sentences.

1. Last year, something unusual happened in my town, which is normally unexciting.

2. According to news reports, a bear had wandered into downtown, and nobody knew where he had come from.

3. The bear, a curious fellow, poked his head into people's yards and ate their fruits and vegetables, particularly enjoying berries.

4. Far from feeling apprehensive, most people hoped to catch a glimpse of this intrepid bear.

5. The bear, who was not afraid of humans, did not feel the need to attack anyone, which was a relief.

6. Animal control, who had been quickly notified, tried to tranquilize the bear, but it was not very effective.

7. After a few days, the bear, seemingly pleased with his little jaunt into downtown, wandered back into the forest and disappeared.

ANSWER KEY

1. ~~Last year,~~ something unusual happened in my town~~, which is normally unexciting~~.

2. ~~According to news reports,~~ a bear had wandered into downtown, and nobody knew where he had come from. **Note: "and nobody knew where he had come from" is not a nonessential comma phrase; it is an independent clause with a subject ("nobody") and verb ("knew"). This shows it *is* important, whereas nonessentials are not important.**

3. The bear~~, a curious fellow,~~ poked his head into people's yards and ate their fruits and vegetables~~, particularly enjoying berries~~.

4. ~~Far from feeling apprehensive,~~ most people hoped to catch a glimpse of this intrepid bear.

5. The bear~~, who was not afraid of humans,~~ did not feel the need to attack anyone~~, which was a relief~~.

6. Animal control~~, who had been quickly notified,~~ tried to tranquilize the bear, but it was not very effective. **Note: "but it was not very effective" is not a nonessential comma phrase; it is an independent clause with a subject ("it") and verb ("was"). This shows it *is* important, whereas nonessentials are not important.**

7. ~~After a few days,~~ the bear~~, seemingly pleased with his little jaunt into downtown,~~ wandered back into the forest and disappeared.

Cross out comma phrases to find the subject for subject-verb agreement

Remember subject-verb agreement questions? They look like this:

The museum, which had received over a million visitors, <u>were</u> honored.

> A) NO CHANGE
>
> B) have been
>
> C) was
>
> D) are

Two things are changing in the answer choices: the verb tense (past/present/etc.) and the number (singular/plural). Let's find the subject and see if it is singular or plural. To do that, we'll follow these steps:

1. Ask who/what was honored?

2. Cross out comma phrases and other distractions.

The museum, ~~which had received over a million visitors~~, <u>were</u> honored.

The subject is "the museum," and as it's just one museum, it's singular. Thus, we need a singular verb, and the only option is C.

To find which answer choice matches a singular subject, we could use any of these methods:

1. Identify what sounds better: "The museum were" vs. "The museum was."

2. Substitute "it" for the singular subject and identify what sounds better: "It were" or "It was."

3. Use the S Rule. (Note that the S Rule is usually only for present tense verbs, but it works for "to be" verbs in the past tense.)

4. Memorize the chart for "to be" verbs in the past tense. (See the "Verbs" chapter.)

Let's try another one:

Few visitors, caught up as they were in trying to focus on the art, <u>has</u> noticed that they painted the walls.

> A) NO CHANGE

B) have

C) is

D) was

Who/what has noticed? What's the subject of "has noticed"? Is the subject singular or plural?

Few visitors, ~~caught up as they were in trying to focus on the art~~, <u>has</u> noticed that they painted the walls.

After crossing out the nonessential comma phrase, we can see that the subject is "few visitors," which is plural. This matches with B, "have noticed."

*For Exercises 2 and 3, you will need to identify prepositions, little grammar words that usually tell you where things are. The most common include **of, with, in, on, over, under, about, from,** and **to**. See the Prepositions chapter for a detailed explanation.*

EXERCISE 2

1. Cross out distractions—nonessentials and prepositional phrases—to find the subject of the **bold** verb. (If there are two **bold** verbs in a sentence, find **both** subjects, one per verb.)

2. Underline the subject and label it singular (s) or plural (pl).

1. Rarely the focus of math or science classes in school, correlation **is** often misunderstood.

2. Correlation, which differs from causation, **is** an important statistical concept.

3. The meaning of correlation **is** a connection between two things or events.

4. The amount of snow, for example, **correlates** with the number of people wearing mittens.

5. When many people **wear** mittens, there **tends** to be a lot of snow.

6. On the other hand, when nobody **wears** mittens, there **is** usually no snow.

7. Therefore, should weather forecasters, after examining the data, **conclude** that wearing mittens **causes** it to snow?

8. No, that **is** a silly idea.

9. Mittens and snow **correlate** but they do not have a causative relationship.

10. In the winter, people in cold climates **are** likely to wear mittens on chilly days.

11. A large amount of snow **may** also fall on cold days.

12. Thus, cold weather, a third variable, **causes** people to wear mittens and snow to accumulate.

13. Mittens and snow **correlate** with each other but do not cause each other.

EXERCISE 3

1. Cross out distractions—nonessentials and prepositional phrases—to find the subject of the **bold** verb. (If there are two **bold** verbs in a sentence, find **both** subjects, one per verb.)

2. Underline the subject and label it singular (s) or plural (pl).

3. Find the correct answer.

1. The photo of the kittens, which I bought last week, <u>is</u> on the wall.

A) NO CHANGE

B) are

C) were

D) have been

2. The bridge between the two towns, New Hope and Lambertville, <u>stretch</u> over a mile.

A) NO CHANGE

B) being stretched

C) are stretching

D) stretches

3. The carrot sticks that have been in the refrigerator since last week <u>is</u> for you.

A) NO CHANGE

B) had been

C) are

D) being

4. Those books on the handmade wooden shelf <u>are</u> heavy.

A) NO CHANGE

B) is

C) has been

D) have been

5. My friends from England, specifically Cambridge and Birmingham, <u>like</u> to drink tea.

A) NO CHANGE

B) liking

C) had liked

D) likes

6. My acquaintances residing in the great state of Delaware <u>likes</u> to drink tea, too.

A) NO CHANGE

B) have been liking

C) has liked

D) like

EXERCISE 2 ANSWER KEY

1. ~~Rarely the focus of math or science classes in school,~~ <u>correlation</u> (s) **is** often misunderstood.

2. <u>Correlation</u> (s)~~, which differs from causation,~~ **is** an important statistical concept.

3. The meaning (s) ~~of correlation~~ **is** a connection ~~between two things or events~~.

4. The amount (s) ~~of snow, for example,~~ **correlates** ~~with the number of people wearing mittens~~.

5. When <u>many people</u> (pl) **wear** mittens, there **tends** to be <u>a lot of snow</u> (s). **Note: "A lot" is the subject, but we can't tell if it's singular or plural without its noun "snow."**

6. ~~On the other hand,~~ when <u>nobody</u> (s) **wears** mittens, there **is** usually <u>no snow</u> (s).

7. ~~Therefore,~~ should weather forecasters~~, after examining the data,~~ **conclude** that <u>wearing</u> (s) mittens **causes** it to snow?

8. No, <u>that</u> (s) **is** a silly idea.

9. <u>Mittens and snow</u> (pl) **correlate** but do not have a causative relationship.

10. ~~In the winter,~~ <u>people</u> (pl) ~~in cold climates~~ **are** likely to wear mittens ~~on chilly days~~.

11. <u>A large amount</u> (s) ~~of snow~~ **may** also fall ~~on cold days~~.

12. ~~Thus,~~ <u>cold weather</u> (s)~~, a third variable,~~ **causes** people to wear mittens and snow to accumulate.

13. <u>Mittens and snow</u> (pl) **correlate** ~~with each other~~ but do not cause each other.

EXERCISE 3 ANSWER KEY

1. A. <u>The photo</u> (s) ~~of the kittens, which I bought last week,~~ <u>is</u> ~~on the wall~~. (Note: You don't really need to cross out "on the wall" because it's nowhere near the subject, but you can if you want to, as it is a prepositional phrase.)

2. D. Oddly enough, <u>the bridge</u> (s) ~~between the two towns, New Hope and Lambertville,~~ <u>stretch</u> ~~over a mile~~. (Note: You don't really need to cross out "over a mile" because it's nowhere near the subject, but you can if you want to, as it is a prepositional phrase.)

3. C. <u>The carrot sticks</u> (pl) (that have been ~~in the refrigerator since last week~~) <u>is</u> ~~for you~~. Note: "that have been...last week" is an *essential* relative clause. Learn more in the Relative Clause chapter! (Note: You don't really need to cross out "for you" because it's nowhere near the subject, but you can if you want to, as it is a prepositional phrase.)

4. A. <u>Those books</u> (pl) ~~on the handmade wooden shelf~~ <u>are</u> heavy.

5. A. <u>My friends</u> (pl) ~~from England, specifically Cambridge and Birmingham,~~ <u>like</u> to drink tea.

6. D. <u>My acquaintances</u> (pl) residing ~~in the great state of Delaware~~ <u>likes</u> to drink tea, too.

COMMA PHRASES STUDY GUIDE!

Write 10 questions in your notebook for this study guide.

STUDY GUIDE ANSWER KEY

Write the answer key on the next page.

Chapter 9: Relative Clauses

Relative clauses are often, but not always, comma phrases. A relative clause will always start with one of the **relative pronouns:**

Which, that, and who/whom/whose

(**When** and **where** can also be relative pronouns, but they are less common.)

Relative clauses are never part of the main core of a sentence and can be crossed out if you want to simplify the sentence. (That is, they aren't independent clauses. More on that later.) You may want to cross out relative clauses to find the main subject of the sentence or to better understand the main idea of a long, confusing sentence.

Here are some examples of sentences using relative clauses. Read them carefully—they're chock-full-o' test tips!

1. The use of relative clauses is an interesting thing **that you can learn about in school**.

2. A relative clause can show up in the middle of a sentence, **which can make the sentence more interesting,** or it can appear at the end of a sentence.

3. English teachers, **who know about this sort of thing,** would not recommend putting a relative clause at the beginning of a sentence.

4. Relative clauses **that give important information** are not surrounded by two commas, whereas those **that give unimportant information** are in a comma phrase, **which is important to remember**.

5. For example, relative clauses using "who," **which are sometimes essential and sometimes nonessential,** may or may not appear as a comma phrase.

6. A relative clause starting with "which" is always a nonessential comma phrase, so it must be surrounded by commas, **which surprises many students.**

7. A relative clause **that starts with "that"** is always essential, so it is never surrounded by commas.

Hot tip: "Which" clauses always have commas. "That" clauses never have commas.

BRAIN DUMP!

Write down as much as you can remember from this chapter. DO THIS FROM MEMORY: DO NOT LOOK AT THE BOOK OR YOUR NOTES. You may want to set a timer for five or ten minutes and write continuously.

EXERCISE 1

1. What are the five main relative pronouns?

2. T/F: A relative clause can stand by itself as a full sentence.

3. T/F: It is impossible to have more than one relative clause in a sentence.

4. T/F: "Which" sometimes takes commas.

5. T/F: "That" clauses never take commas.

6. What is the main difference in meaning between "which" and "that"?

EXERCISE 2

1. Some <u>people, who are unfortunately misguided believe</u> that it is impossible to improve their SAT scores.

A) NO CHANGE

B) people, who are unfortunately misguided, believe

C) people who are unfortunately misguided, believe

D) people, which are unfortunately misguided, believe

2. The reason for this <u>misconception that many people have is</u> interesting.

A) NO CHANGE

B) misconception, that many people have, is

C) misconception, that many people have is

D) misconception that many people have, is

3. Half a century ago, the SAT was very different from the current <u>assessment that, we now all know and love.</u>

A) NO CHANGE

B) assessment, that, we now all know and love.

C) assessment that we, now all know and love.

D) assessment that we now all know and love.

4. The <u>SAT that was taken in the 20th century was</u> indeed difficult to study for, and students found it very challenging to raise their scores.

A) NO CHANGE

B) SAT, that was taken in the 20th century was

C) SAT that was taken in the 20th century, was

D) SAT which was taken in the 20th century was

5. Luckily, the SAT is different now: the new <u>SAT, which you will take is</u> still very challenging, but with hard work and dedication, you can raise your score and learn important skills!

A) NO CHANGE

B) SAT which you will take is

C) SAT, which you will take, is

D) SAT which, you will take, is

CHAPTER 9 ANSWER KEY

EXERCISE 1

1. Which, that, who, whom, whose

2. False. A relative clause is **never** the main core of the sentence.

3. False. There can be more than one. Here's an example: My friend, **who loves to read**, finally bought the book **that she had wanted all month**.

4. False. "Which" clauses **always** take commas.

5. True. "That" is always essential, so it never takes commas.

6. The main difference is that "that" is for something essential, while "which" is for something nonessential. Otherwise, they mean basically the same thing.

EXERCISE 2

1. B. A and C are wrong because they use only one comma. D is wrong because "which" and "that" are for objects, not people.

2. A. "That" does not take commas.

3. D. "That" does not take commas.

4. A. "That" does not take commas. D is wrong because "which" always takes commas.

5. C. "Which" clauses are always surrounded by commas. A and B are wrong because they only use one comma. D is wrong because the comma should go before "which."

RELATIVE CLAUSE STUDY GUIDE!

Write 10 questions in your notebook for this study guide.

STUDY GUIDE ANSWER KEY

Write the answer key on the next page.

Chapter 10: Who vs. Whom

Read through the sample sentences, noticing patterns in the CORRECT vs. the INCORRECT sentences. Then try to fill in the blanks for the who vs. whom rules:

Rule of thumb: Use "whom" instead of "who" when _____ comes before (or sometimes at the end of a sentence). Never use "whom" when the next word is a _____.

1. CORRECT: This is my friend who plays the guitar.

2. CORRECT: Who said that?

3. CORRECT: To whom did you speak?

4. CORRECT: Is this the girl for whom you bought that gift?

5. CORRECT: Is this the girl whom you bought that gift for?

6. CORRECT: Do you know to whom you are speaking?

7. CORRECT: Do you know whom you are speaking to?

8. CORRECT: Be careful around whom you say that.

9. CORRECT: Be careful whom you say that around.

10. WRONG: This is my brother whom plays the drums.

11. WRONG: She is the one whom saw me at the dance.

12. WRONG: For who did you buy this gift?

13. WRONG: Who did you buy this gift for?

Ready for the answer?

Use "whom" instead of "who" when a preposition comes before (or sometimes at the end of a sentence). Never use "whom" when the next word is a verb.

Why?

"Who" is a subject. "Whom" is an object.

Hot tip: Grammatically, "who" can be used when "he" can be used, and "whom" can be used when "him" can be used.

Check out these examples:

My brother is the one **who** plays guitar.

He plays guitar.

My dad is someone **whom** I really admire.

I really admire **him**.

Notice that "who" is immediately followed by a verb, while "whom" is immediately followed by a noun or pronoun subject.

"Whom" is also the object in a prepositional phrase, just as "him" or "her" would be. Consider:

To whom did you write a letter?

I wrote a letter **to him**.

Is that the person **about whom** I've been hearing so much?

I've been hearing so much **about him**.

BRAIN DUMP!

Write down as much as you can remember from this chapter. DO THIS FROM MEMORY: DO NOT LOOK AT THE BOOK OR YOUR NOTES. You may want to set a timer for five or ten minutes and write continuously.

EXERCISE

Decide if each sentence is correct or incorrect. Fix it if needed.

1. To whom did you speak?

2. Whom called you yesterday?

3. My mom is a lady whom loves shopping.

4. About who are you speaking?

5. Mary is the one whom I called.

6. Sam is the one who called me.

7. Sean was the first person who I told.

8. Shauna was the first person who told me.

ANSWER KEY

1. Correct

2. Incorrect. It should say "who" because "who" is the subject of "called."

3. Incorrect. It should say "who" because "who" is the subject of "loves."

4. Incorrect. It should say "whom" because "whom" is the object of the preposition "about"; "you" is the subject.

5. Correct

6. Correct

7. Incorrect. It should say "whom" because "whom" is the object; I told *him*.

8. Correct.

WHO VS. WHOM STUDY GUIDE!

Write 10 questions in your notebook for this study guide.

STUDY GUIDE ANSWER KEY

Write the answer key on the next page.

Chapter 11: Parts of Speech: Adjectives & Adverbs

Adjectives

Adjectives describe nouns (or pronouns).

Here are some adjectives: cool, warm, big, small, blue, red, interesting, boring, fun, tired, short, tall.

If you're not sure if something is an adjective, try this trick: substitute the word "cool" and see if the sentence still works grammatically. Check it out:

1. I saw an **interesting** movie yesterday. → I saw a **cool** movie yesterday. ("Interesting" is an adjective here.)

2. The dog is **brown**. → The dog is **cool**. ("Brown" is an adjective here.)

3. Look at that **wooden** table. → Look at that **cool** table. ("Wooden" is an adjective here.)

Alternatively, you can just think of adjectives as words that describe nouns.

Adverbs

Adverbs describe verbs, adjectives, or other adverbs. **They usually end in "ly."**

Here are some adverbs: really, very, largely, interestingly, quickly, slowly.

Hot tip: The SAT/ACT may use adjectives where adverbs belong.

Keep an eye out for anything like this:

The car drove <u>slow.</u>

- A) NO CHANGE
- B) too slow.
- C) slowly.
- D) real slow.

"Slow" describes how it "drove," which is a verb. We need an adverb—so, probably something ending in "ly." Only option C contains an adverb, so C is correct.

BRAIN DUMP!

Write down as much as you can remember from this chapter. DO THIS FROM MEMORY: DO NOT LOOK AT THE BOOK OR YOUR NOTES. You may want to set a timer for five or ten minutes and write continuously.

EXERCISE 1

1. I want to stay in bed; I don't feel <u>good</u> today.

    - A) NO CHANGE
    - B) well
    - C) exquisite
    - D) magnanimous

2. Hurry up! You're walking too <u>slow</u>!

    - A) NO CHANGE
    - B) slower

C) quick

D) slowly

3. Few people do research as <u>carefully</u> as she does.

    A) NO CHANGE

    B) careful

    C) equally careful

    D) much with care

4. Few people do <u>careful</u> research like she does.

    A) NO CHANGE

    B) carefully

    C) with care

    D) caring

5. This pizza is really <u>good</u>.

    A) NO CHANGE

    B) goodly

    C) well

    D) greatly

EXERCISE 2

Sentence mapping, revisited: Circle (or **bold**) all nouns. <u>Underline</u> all verbs. Label (or comment) all adverbs and adjectives.

1. The horse whinnied nervously.

2. John spent all morning looking for his keys.

3. Sam laughed because she had hidden John's keys very effectively.

4. Summer is the hottest season.

5. My guinea pigs are always squeaking loudly.

CHAPTER 11 ANSWER KEY

EXERCISE 1

1. B. "Well" modifies the verb "feel," so an adverb is needed.

2. D. "Slowly" modifies the verb "are walking," so an adverb is needed.

3. A. "Carefully" modifies the verb phrase "do research," so an adverb is needed.

4. A. "Careful" describes the research, which is a noun, so an adjective is needed.

5. A. "Good" describes the noun "pizza," so an adjective is needed.

EXERCISE 2

1. Nouns: horse. Verbs: whinnied. Adverbs: nervously.

2. Nouns: John; morning; keys. Verbs: spent (NOT looking). No adverbs or adjectives.

3. Nouns: Sam; keys (or John's keys. NOT just John). Verbs: laughed; had hidden. Adverbs: very; effectively

4. Nouns: summer; season. Verbs: is. Adjectives: hottest.

5. Nouns: guinea pigs (or my guinea pigs. NOT just my). Verbs: are (or are squeaking. NOT just squeaking). Adverbs: loudly.

ADJECTIVES AND ADVERBS STUDY GUIDE!

Write 10 questions in your notebook for this study guide.

STUDY GUIDE ANSWER KEY

Write the answer key on the next page.

Chapter 12: Articles

Articles are those little words: a, an, the.

"The" is used for something specific. If your teacher says, "Have you read the book?" you will probably feel nervous and wonder if there is some specific book that was assigned. "The book" indicates there is some book that your teacher already told you about. It begs the question, "What book? Am I supposed to know about this already?"

It would be quite different if your teacher had asked, "Have you read a book?" In that situation, she is simply asking whether you have ever read any book. "A" and "an" refer to things in general, not to some specific item that you talked about already.

That's pretty much it. Other things can act like articles:

<u>The</u> book is on the shelf.

<u>A</u> book is on the shelf.

<u>My</u> book is on the shelf.

<u>Your</u> book is on the shelf.

"My" and "your" are technically possessives, not articles, but they **act exactly like articles**. Here's another example:

<u>Michael's</u> book is on the shelf.

Functionally, this is almost the same sentence as "the book is on the shelf." Is Michael on the shelf? No, his book is. Again, "Michael's" is a possessive acting **exactly the same as an article.**

BRAIN DUMP!

Write down as much as you can remember from this chapter. DO THIS FROM MEMORY: DO NOT LOOK AT THE BOOK OR YOUR NOTES. You may want to set a timer for five or ten minutes and write continuously.

EXERCISE

Circle (or bold) the correct article.

1. The/a homework assignment discussed earlier is on the/a board.

2. I just thought of the/an idea. Want to hear it?

3. She created the/a most famous painting of all time.

4. He wrote the/a famous poem that many students read in school.

5. There is the/a famous play about an evil king.

6. Did you listen to the/a podcast I recommended yesterday?

1. the; the (one specific assignment on one specific board, both of which have been previously discussed or known about)

2. an (some idea that has not been discussed yet)

3. the (one specific painting)

4. a (some poem that has not been discussed yet)

5. a (some play that has not been discussed yet)

6. the (one specific podcast that was discussed yesterday)

ARTICLES MINI STUDY GUIDE!

Write 5 questions in your notebook for this mini study guide.

STUDY GUIDE ANSWER KEY

Write the answer key on the next page.

INTERLEAVING PRACTICE TEST 1

This test includes all grammar question types in Part 2 of the book thus far.

Excerpt from *The Elements of Style*, by William Strunk. It has been altered slightly.

Begin each paragraph with a topic sentence and end it in conformity with the beginning

Again, the object is to aid the reader. The practice here recommended enables (1) <u>the reader</u> to discover the purpose of each paragraph as he (2) <u>began</u> to read it, and to retain this purpose in mind as he ends it. For this reason, the most generally useful kind of paragraph, particularly in exposition and argument, (3) <u>being</u> that in which the topic sentence comes at or near the beginning, the succeeding sentences explain or develop the (4) <u>statement, that was made</u> in (5) <u>a</u> topic sentence, and the (6) <u>final</u> sentence either (7) <u>emphasized</u> the thought of the topic sentence or states some important consequence.

Ending with a digression, or with an unimportant detail, is particularly to be avoided. If the paragraph (8) <u>forming</u> part of a larger composition, its relation to what precedes, or its function as a part of the whole, may need to be expressed. This can sometimes be done by (9) <u>a word or phrase</u> in the topic sentence. Sometimes, however, it is expedient to precede the topic sentence by one or more sentences of introduction or transition. If more than one such sentence (10) <u>were</u> required, it is generally better (11) <u>sets</u> apart the transitional sentences as a separate paragraph.

1. A) NO CHANGE

   B) it

   C) them

   D) those

2. A) NO CHANGE

   B) begins

   C) beginning

   D) begin

3. A) NO CHANGE

   B) is

   C) are

   D) have been

4. A) NO CHANGE

   B) statement was made

   C) statement made

   D) made

5. A) NO CHANGE

   B) the

   C) those

   D) some

6. A) NO CHANGE

   B) finally

C) finite

D) finitely

7. A) NO CHANGE

    B) emphasizing

    C) emphasize

    D) emphasizes

8. A) NO CHANGE

    B) had formed

    C) being formed

    D) forms

9. A) NO CHANGE

    B) that

    C) those which are

    D) this

10. A) NO CHANGE

    B) are

    C) is

    D) was

11. A) NO CHANGE

    B) to set

    C) of setting

    D) have set

INTERLEAVING PRACTICE TEST 4 ANSWER KEY

1. A. "The reader" makes it clear who is being discussed. It would be possible to use a pronoun to refer to the singular "reader" in the previous sentence, but B is wrong because "it" can not refer to a person, and C and D are wrong because they are plural.

2. B. The subject is the singular "he." We can tell that we need the present tense because the sentence says "enables" and "ends" in the present tense.

3. B. If we cross out all non-essential comma phrases and prepositional phrases, we see that the subject is "the most generally useful kind," which is singular, matching "is." In addition, we need the present tense because the other verb in the sentence is "comes."

4. C. A is wrong because "that" clauses do not use commas. D is wrong because it cuts out an important word, "statement." Note that although shorter is usually better, we still have to be careful that a shorter answer does not omit anything important.

5. B. Notice that earlier in the sentence, it says "the topic sentence," and this is repeated again later in the sentence.

6. A. "Final" is an adjective describing the noun "sentence."

7. D. The subject is the singular "sentence," which matches "emphasizes." It matches the tense of "states;" in fact, they are in parallel construction, so it is essential that they match: "either emphasizes...or states." (For more on this check out the Parallelism chapter.)

8. D. The subject is the singular "paragraph," and it matches the tenses later in the sentence and in the next sentences: "precedes," "may need," "can," and "is." There is no indication that the past perfect tense is required; it is usually wrong.

9. A. B, C, and D are too vague.

10. C. The subject is the singular "more than one sentence," so we can cross out A and B. It must be present tense because the other verb in the sentence is "is."

11. B. "It is...better to set" is the correct use of "better to."

Chapter 13: Indefinite Pronouns

Indefinite pronouns are difficult to describe and much easier to demonstrate. Here are some indefinite pronouns:

Anyone, everyone, something, nothing, nobody, somebody.

Unlike a normal pronoun (like "he" or "she"), indefinite pronouns don't refer to any particular antecedent.

They tend to show up on the SAT/ACT in questions about subject-verb agreement. This is because we colloquially use indefinite pronouns very differently from how the test uses them.

These are the singular/plural rules for indefinite pronouns according to the test's Standard Academic American English rules:

Hint: As you read down the column of singular indefinite pronouns, look for patterns.

Singular	Plural	It depends on the noun
another	a number	all
anybody	both	any
anyone	few	most
anything	many	none
each		some
either*, neither*		
every		
everybody		
everyone		
everything		
noone		
nobody		
somebody		
someone		
something		

Give this challenge a shot:

Write down any patterns in your notebook:

Indefinite pronouns are singular if they start with _____

and **if they end with _____.**

Answer:

Indefinite pronouns are singular if they start with **every, any,** and **some,** and if they end with **one, body,** and **thing,** (or **ther,** as in either/neither).

Based on the patterns, let's rewrite that chart in a better way:

Singular	Plural	It depends on the noun
any-	a number	all
every-	both	any
some-	few	most
-body	many	none
-one		some
-thing		
each		
either*, neither*		
another		

Hot tip: **Each** and **every** are singular. Memorize this!

*Note:

"Either" and "neither" are usually, but not always, singular. On the test, they are usually singular.

Here are some examples with the verb **in bold**:

1. Either my brother or my sister **has** been stealing my dessert each night.

2. Either pizza or ice cream **sounds** good to me.

3. Neither the dog nor the cat **looks** like it has had a bath recently.

This makes some logical sense: Either my brother or sister has stolen my dessert, and I don't know which one, but it's not both of them. Thus, the singular makes sense here. (It makes a bit less sense with "neither," but the rule still sticks.)

But.

On some rare occasions, we might want to compare two things that are **not** singular. In this case, the verb hugs whatever noun is closest to it and, like a chameleon, changes to match the number that it's next to.

Check it out:

4. Either my friends or <u>my cousins</u> **are** coming over to visit.

5. Either my aunt or <u>her children</u> **are** allergic to chocolate, but I can't remember which.

6. Neither the dog nor <u>the kittens **seem**</u> nervous about their new home.

Nonetheless, **either and neither are usually singular** because they are usually used to compare two singular things (like in sentences 1-3).

What about "It depends on the noun"?

These words simply take the number of their nouns. For example, consider "most."

"Most" can be plural if its noun is plural: **I ate most of the <u>cupcakes</u>.**

"Most" can be singular if its noun is singular: **I drank most of the <u>water</u>.**

Try this problem:

Most of the cupcakes <u>are in my stomach</u> because I ate them.

A) NO CHANGE

B) is in my stomach

C) will be in my stomach

D) being in my stomach

What is the subject? Ask "What's in my stomach?" Most of the cupcakes. This is plural because most of the cupcakes constitutes more than one. A is the answer. It can't be C because "I ate them" is in the past tense, while C is in the future tense. It can't be D because "being" is usually wrong, and "being" is a gerund, not a main verb.

What about this one?

Most of the water <u>are in my stomach</u> because I drank it all.

A) NO CHANGE

B) is in my stomach

C) will be in my stomach

D) being in my stomach

What is the subject—what is in my stomach? Most of the water. This is singular; it isn't many waters, it's just one thing: water. The answer is B.

(Fun fact: "Water" is what we call an "uncountable noun" because it tends to stay singular no matter how much of it we're talking about; you generally can't say "I drank two waters," instead saying "I drank a lot of water." There are lots of uncountable nouns, including rice, juice, milk, soda, and more.)

BRAIN DUMP!

Write down as much as you can remember from this chapter. DO THIS FROM MEMORY: DO NOT LOOK AT THE BOOK OR YOUR NOTES. You may want to set a timer for five or ten minutes and write continuously.

EXERCISE 1

Fill in the blanks in the chart. Do as much as you can from memory, then check your answers.

Singular	Plural	It depends on the noun
another	a number	_____
anybody	_____	_____
_____	few	_____

_____	many	none
each		some
either*, _____*		
every		
_____		
everyone		
_____		
noone		
_____		
somebody		
_____		
_____		

EXERCISE 2

1. Each student always <u>arrive</u> on time.

    A) NO CHANGE

    B) arrives

    C) were arriving

    D) have arrived

2. Everyone on the girls' basketball team brought <u>they're</u> own water bottle.

A) NO CHANGE

B) their

C) one's

D) her

3. All the kids in the room ate <u>his or her</u> lunch.

A) NO CHANGE

B) they're

C) their

D) one's own

4. Every dog, no matter how big, small, young, or old, <u>are</u> adorable and worthy of love.

A) NO CHANGE

B) were

C) have been

D) is

5. Neither the hamster nor the guinea pig <u>were able to</u> speak fluent French.

A) NO CHANGE

B) are able to

C) has been able to

D) have been able to

6. Despite my pets' inability to learn foreign languages, both <u>are</u> actually quite intelligent.

A) NO CHANGE

B) is

C) having been

D) had been

7. Nobody <u>thinks</u> my pets are capable of becoming bilingual.

    A) NO CHANGE

    B) have thought

    C) think

    D) had thought

8. Is there anyone out there who <u>believing</u> in my guinea pig and hamster?

    A) NO CHANGE

    B) believes

    C) believe

    D) belief

CHAPTER 13 ANSWER KEY

EXERCISE 1

See the first chart earlier in this chapter.

EXERCISE 2

1. B. "Each student" is the subject. "Each" is singular.

2. D. This is a trick: "They're" is short for "they are," so it needs to change to a possessive. However, B is wrong because "everyone" is singular.

3. C. "All the kids" is the subject. "All" is plural because "kids" is plural.

4. D. "Every dog" is the subject. "Every" is singular.

5. C. "Neither" is singular.

6. A. "Both" is plural.

7. A. "Nobody" is singular.

8. B. "Anyone" is singular.

INDEFINITE PRONOUNS STUDY GUIDE!

Write 10 questions in your notebook for this study guide.

STUDY GUIDE ANSWER KEY

Write the answer key on the next page.

Chapter 14: Dashes for Nonessentials

Remember nonessential comma phrases, which use two commas to separate out an unimportant idea? Well, two dashes can do that, too. In general, dashes are less common than commas and typically indicate longer or more dramatic pauses. Dashes can stand in for other punctuation, too; you can use a dash instead of a colon or use dashes instead of commas around a nonessential.

Hot tip: Two dashes can be used in place of two commas to separate a nonessential phrase. You cannot, however, mix and match one dash with one comma.

Both of these sentences are correct:

1. My friend, who went to the beach last summer, tends to come to school sunburned.

2. My friend—who went to the beach last summer—tends to come to school sunburned.

They both say the same thing and include a nonessential; Sentence 1 uses two commas, and Sentence 2 uses two dashes for the nonessential.

Sentence 3, however, is incorrect:

X 3. My friend, who went to the beach last summer—tends to come to school sunburned.

This sentence is wrong because it uses one comma and one dash to offset a nonessential, but they need to match.

BRAIN DUMP!

Write down as much as you can remember from this chapter. DO THIS FROM MEMORY: DO NOT LOOK AT THE BOOK OR YOUR NOTES. You may want to set a timer for five or ten minutes and write continuously.

EXERCISE

1. The girl, a basketball player—had little free time.

A) NO CHANGE

B) player, had

C) player had

D) player; had

2. The dog—which lives across the street, is dangerously fluffy.

A) NO CHANGE

B) dog, it

C) dog, which

D) dog; which

3. The hors d'oeuvres—an unpalatable combination of caviar and cream cheese—were not a hit among the guests.

A) NO CHANGE

B) cheese; were

C) cheese were

D) cheese, were

4. I had never seen a penguin in a fabulous hat before—penguins usually don't wear anything, let alone foppish headwear.

A) NO CHANGE

B) anything let

C) anything—let

D) anything; let

5. The mysterious document, which we read carefully—after ensuring we were alone—by candlelight, contained a secret map.

A) NO CHANGE

B) document, which we read carefully, after

C) document—which we read carefully—after

D) document which we read carefully after

6. I love sushi—I would walk miles for a good tuna avocado sushi roll.

A) NO CHANGE

B) sushi, I

C) sushi. And I

D) sushi; and I

ANSWER KEY

1. B. "A basketball player" is a nonessential starting with a comma, so it must end with a comma, too.

2. C. "Which lives across the street" is a nonessential ending with a comma, so it must start with a comma, too.

3. A. "An unpalatable combination of caviar and cream cheese" is a nonessential starting with a dash, so it must end with a dash, too.

4. A. The dash after "before" marks a long pause between two ideas; it splits the sentence into two halves. "Let alone foppish headwear" is a nonessential. It starts with a comma and ends at the end of the sentence.

5. A. There are two nonessentials, one nested inside the other. ", Which we read carefully...by candlelight," is one nonessential; since it ends with a comma, it must also start with a

comma. "—After ensuring we were alone—" is another nonessential; since it ends with a dash, it must also start with a dash.

6. A. The dash indicates a dramatic pause between two ideas. Option B is wrong because it is a run-on sentence; both halves are independent clauses. Options C and D are both the same because a period and semicolon are exactly the same on the SAT. They can't both be right, so they must both be wrong. In addition, a period FANBOYS or semicolon FANBOYS is always wrong. To learn more, read the Clauses chapter.

DASHES STUDY GUIDE!

Write 10 questions in your notebook for this study guide.

STUDY GUIDE ANSWER KEY

Write the answer key on the next page.

Chapter 15: Clauses and Punctuation

What's a clause?

You tell me.

Use these two lists of clauses and non-clauses to fill in the blanks:

Every clause has a _____ and a _____.

Clause	Not a clause
I like pizza.	Like pizza.
Those pickles look a bit moldy.	Those pickles.
Before she got home,	Before she,

Ready for the answer?

Every clause has a <u>subject</u> and a <u>verb</u>.

You may have also noticed that in the first two examples, but not in the third example, the clause forms a full sentence. This is because there are two types of clauses: **independent clauses** and **dependent clauses**.

Use these examples to fill in the blanks:

_____ clauses can stand alone as full sentences.

_____ clauses can not be full sentences by themselves.

Independent Clause	Dependent Clause
I like pizza	Although I like pizza
Those pickles look a bit moldy	Because those pickles look a bit moldy
She got home early	When she got home early

Ready for the answer?

Independent clauses can stand alone as full sentences.

Dependent clauses can not be full sentences by themselves.

Note: Dependent clauses are also called subordinate clauses. They are the same thing.

Subordinating conjunctions

Did you notice that all the dependent clauses started with something other than the subject? **Although, because,** and **when** are examples of **subordinating conjunctions**, affectionately known as "subordinators" or "SWABIs."

Why "SWABI"? I'm glad you asked! SWABI is a mnemonic to help students remember some of the most common subordinating conjunctions:

Since

When

After
Because

If

In addition to these, there are many more subordinating conjunctions:

Although, as, before, even though, once, unless, while…

and many more.

You should memorize or learn to recognize all of these subordinating conjunctions.

Hot tip: Subordinating conjunctions appear at the **beginning** of a clause, and they make it dependent.

Coordinating conjunctions: FANBOYS

Coordinating conjunctions, also known as FANBOYS, are special. There are only seven of them, and they are the only words that can link two independent clauses. They are:

For

And

Nor
But

Or

Yet

So

That's it. There are no other words that can link two independent clauses. If you want to link two independent clauses, you need for, and, nor, but, or, yet, or so.

Note that **to connect two independent clauses,** you must use **a comma** followed by a **FANBOYS.**

To put it another way,

Ind ,FANBOYS Ind

Here's what that looks like in a sentence:

1. I tried the sandwich**, but** I didn't like it.

2. She practiced the piano**, and** he practiced the cello.

3. My dog likes long walks**, and** my cat likes to knock things over.

4. We can go to the mall**, or** we can stay at home.

5. I don't want to go to the mall**, nor** do I want to stay at home.

Hot tip: "And" and "but" are the most common FANBOYS.

"For" is actually not usually used as a FANBOYS, joining two independent clauses. In fact, using "for" as a FANBOYS kind of makes you sound like an ancient king:

This is my favorite sword**, for** it has vanquished many foes!

Tonight, we feast**, for** we have won the battle!

I am grateful**,** **for** you have saved my life.

See what I mean? "For" is almost never used as a FANBOYS in modern times.

Usually, "for" is used as a **preposition**:

This gift is **for you**.

I have a message **for her**.

Hot tip: "For" is almost always a preposition, NOT a FANBOYS.

So why do we still have "for" on the FANBOYS list?

Well, if we didn't, then it would only say ANBOYS, and that's not very catchy.

BRAIN DUMP!

Write down as much as you can remember from this chapter. DO THIS FROM MEMORY: DO NOT LOOK AT THE BOOK OR YOUR NOTES. You may want to set a timer for five or ten minutes and write continuously.

EXERCISE 1

1. What are the coordinating conjunctions? Write the word next to its first letter:

F

A

N

B

O

Y

S

2. What are some of the common subordinating conjunctions? Write the word next to its first letter:

S

W

A

B

I

3. What is the difference between coordinating and subordinating conjunctions? What clauses are they associated with?

EXERCISE 2

What kind of clause is it? Circle "IND" for independent or "DEP" for dependent. Some sentences will have two clauses.

1. Studying is important. IND/DEP

2. However, it is also important to study the right way. IND/DEP

3. Because the brain learns through repetition (IND/DEP), reviewing notes and old quizzes is a great technique. IND/DEP

4. While repetition is important (IND/DEP), it is not the only thing that matters. IND/DEP

5. Since the brain learns best through retrieval (IND/DEP), students learn the most by testing themselves with flashcards, practice tests, and review games. IND/DEP

6. It can be difficult to make and use flashcards (IND/DEP), but it is worth the trouble. IND/DEP

EXERCISE 3

Here are some grammatically correct phrases. Let's add a subject and verb to transform them into clauses!

It does **not** need to be a full sentence.

Example: Phrase: After seeing the movie,   Clause: *After I saw the movie,*

This is missing a subject and a main verb ("ing" gerunds are not main verbs).

1. Phrase: While watching a movie,   Clause:

2. Phrase: Singing quietly,   Clause:

3. Phrase: Before doing my homework,   Clause:

4. Phrase: Having already read the book,   Clause:

Now turn these clauses into phrases by taking away the subject and main verb. There is more than one correct answer.

Example: Clause: Since the cat felt grumpy,   Phrase: *Feeling grumpy,*

5. Clause: Because the dog felt hungry,   Phrase:

6. Clause: While my phone charged,   Phrase:

7. Clause: As the bell rang,   Phrase:

8. Clause: Although the fog was thick,   Phrase:

EXERCISE 4

In this exercise, you will label the parts of two-part sentences. You'll see these sentences again in the next chapter, so pay close attention. Follow these steps for each sentence:

1. Label the subject, verb, and subordinating conjunction (if any).

2. Circle CLAUSE or NOT A COMPLETE CLAUSE.

3. Fill in the blank with DEP (for dependent) or IND (for independent).

Example:

The disgruntled turtle slowly turned around

because he thought that he had smelled food.

First part subject: **turtle**

First part verb: **turned**

Second part subject: **he**

Second part verb: **thought**

Subordinating conjunction: **because**

The first part is **IND clause**. The second part is **DEP clause**.

1. The strapping young fellow decided to try his luck

he shot the bullet at the target.

First part subject: _____

First part verb: _____

Second part subject: _____

Second part verb: _____

Subordinating conjunction, if any: _____

The first part is _____ clause/not a complete clause. The second part is _____ clause/not a complete clause.

2. The frightened dog pondered his past

and decided never to return.

First part subject: _____

First part verb: _____

Second part subject: _____

Second part verb: _____

Subordinating conjunction, if any: _____

The first part is _____ clause/not a complete clause. The second part is _____ clause/not a complete clause.

3. After I ate dinner

I considered watching a movie.

First part subject: _____

First part verb: _____

Second part subject: _____

Second part verb: _____

Subordinating conjunction, if any: _____

The first part is _____ clause/not a complete clause. The second part is _____ clause/not a complete clause.

4. I was tired

I went to bed.

First part subject: _____

First part verb: _____

Second part subject: _____

Second part verb: _____

Subordinating conjunction, if any: _____

The first part is _____ clause/not a complete clause. The second part is _____ clause/not a complete clause.

CHAPTER 15 ANSWER KEY

EXERCISE 1

1. For, And, Nor, But, Or, Yet, So

2. Since, When (or While), After (or Although), Because (or Before), If

3. Coordinating conjunctions are FANBOYS. A comma FANBOYS separates two independent clauses. Subordinating conjunctions are SWABIs. A subordinating conjunction goes at the beginning of a clause to make it dependent.

EXERCISE 2

1. Studying is important. **IND**/DEP

2. However, it is also important to study the right way. **IND**/DEP (Note: "However" is a non-essential comma phrase, NOT a subordinating conjunction. Subordinating conjunctions are never directly followed by a comma like that.)

3. Because the brain learns through repetition (IND/**DEP**), reviewing notes and old quizzes is a great technique. **IND**/DEP

4. While repetition is important (IND/**DEP**), it is not the only thing that matters. **IND**/DEP

5. Since the brain learns best through retrieval (IND/**DEP**), students learn the most by testing themselves with flashcards, practice tests, and review games. **IND**/DEP

6. It can be difficult to make and use flashcards (**IND**/DEP), but it is worth the trouble. **IND**/DEP (Note: Remember that "but" is a FANBOYS, connecting two independent clauses.

EXERCISE 3

(Some variation is expected; these are suggested answers)

Part 1:

1. Phrase: While watching a movie,   Clause: **While I was watching a movie,**

2. Phrase: Singing quietly,   Clause: **When I was singing quietly,**

3. Phrase: Before doing my homework,   Clause: **Before I did my homework,**

4. Phrase: Having already read the book,   Clause: **Because I had already read the book,**

Part 2:

5. Clause: Because the dog felt hungry,   Phrase: **Feeling hungry,**

6. Clause: While my phone charged,   Phrase: **With my phone charging,**

7. Clause: As the bell rang,   Phrase: **Bell ringing,**

8. Clause: Although the fog was thick,   Phrase: **Despite the thick fog,**

EXERCISE 4

1. The strapping young fellow decided to try his luck

he shot the bullet at the target.

First part subject: **The strapping young fellow**

First part verb: **decided**

Second part subject: **he**

Second part verb: **shot**

Subordinating conjunction, if any: **(none)**

The first part is **IND clause**/not a complete clause. The second part is **IND clause**/not a complete clause.

2. The frightened dog pondered his past

and decided never to return.

First part subject: **The frightened dog**

First part verb: **pondered**

Second part subject: **(none)**

Second part verb: **decided**

Subordinating conjunction, if any: **(none; "and" is a FANBOYS)**

The first part is **IND clause**/not a complete clause. The second part is
_____ clause/**not a complete clause (it is missing a subject)**.

3. After I ate dinner

I considered watching a movie.

First part subject: **I**

First part verb: **ate**

Second part subject: **I**

Second part verb: **considered**

Subordinating conjunction, if any: **After**

The first part is **DEP clause**/not a complete clause. The second part is **IND clause**/not a complete clause.

4. I was tired

I went to bed.

First part subject: **I**

First part verb: **was**

Second part subject: **I**

Second part verb: **went**

Subordinating conjunction, if any: **(none)**

The first part is **IND clause**/not a complete clause. The second part is **IND clause**/not a complete clause.

CLAUSES AND CONJUNCTIONS STUDY GUIDE!

Write 10 questions in your notebook for this study guide.

STUDY GUIDE ANSWER KEY

Write the answer key on the next page.

Chapter 16: Clause Punctuation Rules

Answers that are always wrong

Hot tip: . FANBOYS and ; FANBOYS are (almost) always wrong.

A period followed by a FANBOYS, as well as a semicolon followed by a FANBOYS, is always wrong. Have you ever heard a teacher tell you not to start a sentence with "and"? It's the same thing: traditionally, you shouldn't start a new sentence with a FANBOYS.

In real life, authors do this all the time, and you may even see it happen on the Reading test. On grammar questions, though, never use a FANBOYS after a period or semicolon–unless the semicolon is separating a long list, rather than starting a new sentence.

Check out this confusing sentence as an example:

> X I want to visit Paris, France, Tokyo, Japan, and London, England.

Look how many commas there are, and how confusing it is! Let's try switching to semicolons to clarify things:

> I want to visit Paris, France; Tokyo, Japan; and London, England.

Even though there is a semicolon followed by "and," this sentence is **correct**. The semicolons help separate the list items. Do you agree that this version of the sentence is less confusing?

Hot tip: "Being" is pretty much always wrong.

The SAT and ACT, as well as many English teachers, dislike the word "being."

Hot tip: "However" in the middle of a sentence is pretty much always wrong. When you see

---

"however" on the SAT/ACT, it probably needs a period or semicolon next to it.

The SAT/ACT typically uses "however" and other transition words to hide a run-on sentence. It should usually go at the beginning, or sometimes at the end, of a sentence. That said, it is possible to put "however" in the middle of a sentence—it's just that the SAT/ACT usually doesn't.

Independent + independent

To separate **two independent clauses**, use a comma FANBOYS (,FANBOYS), period, or semicolon. According to the SAT/ACT, a period and semicolon are **the same thing**. (In real life, a semicolon is used just like a period, but it separates two sentences that are closely related.)

Let me repeat that:

Hot tip: A period and semicolon are the same thing.

To put it pseudo-mathematically,

. = ; = ,FANBOYS

That is, these are all grammatically identical:

1. I like chicken. My brother likes fish.

2. I like chicken; my brother likes fish.

3. I like chicken, and my brother likes fish.

On the SAT/ACT, this allows you to cross out answer choices if they are grammatically identical; two answers can't both be right, so they must both be wrong. Here's an example:

Potatoes are my favorite <u>vegetable; because</u> they are very versatile.

A) NO CHANGE

B) vegetable. Because

C) vegetable, and because

D) vegetable because

Option A uses a semicolon, option B uses a period, and option C uses a comma FANBOYS. Grammatically, these are all the same, so we can cross them all out. We are left with only one option: D, which is the correct answer.

Independent + dependent

Remember dependent clauses? Those clauses that can't stand alone because they start with a subordinating conjunction like "since," "while," "because," or "although"?

A dependent clause must use a comma if followed by an independent clause. That is,

DEP , IND

Example:

Because I was hungry, I ate some fries.

However, if we change the order of the clauses, the comma disappears. That is,

IND DEP (no comma)

Example:

I ate some fries because I was hungry.

Hot tip: DEP , IND

IND DEP (no comma)

This is because a comma represents a pause in speech. Try reading these two sentences aloud and notice where you naturally pause:

Because I was hungry, I ate some fries.

I ate some fries because I was hungry.

You probably paused naturally where the comma was. Either way, you should memorize the above comma rules.

BRAIN DUMP!

Write down as much as you can remember from this chapter. DO THIS FROM MEMORY: DO NOT LOOK AT THE BOOK OR YOUR NOTES. You may want to set a timer for five or ten minutes and write continuously.

EXERCISE 1

1. Write down all three ways to separate two independent clauses:

    1.

    2.

    3.

2. Add a comma to complete the two comma rules for dependent clauses:

1. Dep ind

2. Ind dep

EXERCISE 2

In the previous chapter, you identified the types of clauses in these sentences. Now, do that again, and use that clause information to answer the test-style punctuation questions.

First, label the subject, verb, and subordinating conjunction, and circle CLAUSE or NOT A COMPLETE CLAUSE. Second, fill in the blank with DEP or IND (or nothing, if it's not a complete clause). Finally, choose the correct answer choice based on your punctuation rules.

1. The strapping young fellow decided to try his <u>luck, he</u> shot the bullet at the target.

The first part is _____ clause/not a complete clause. The second part is _____ clause/not a complete clause.

   A. NO CHANGE

   B. luck; and he

   C. luck; he

   D. luck. And he

2. The frightened dog pondered his <u>past, and</u> decided never to return.

The first part is _____ clause/not a complete clause. The second part is _____ clause/not a complete clause.

   A. NO CHANGE

   B. past; and

C. past and he

D. past and

3. After I ate <u>dinner, I</u> considered watching a movie.

The first part is _____ clause/not a complete clause. The second part is _____ clause/not a complete clause.

A. NO CHANGE

B. dinner I

C. dinner, and I

D. dinner; I

4. <u>I was</u> tired, I went to bed.

The first part is _____ clause/not a complete clause. The second part is _____ clause/not a complete clause.

A. NO CHANGE

B. When I was

C. Being that I was

D. I felt

EXERCISE 3

Based on the rules for what answers are always wrong, cross out some answer choices. Cross out at least one option per question.

1.

A) thirsty. She

B) thirsty; she

C) thirsty, she

D) thirsty, so she

2.

A) difficult; all

B) difficult, and all

C) difficult, being all

D) difficult all

3.

A) meals, but I later

B) meals, however I later

C) meals. But I later

D) meals; but I later

4.

A) it; I knew

B) it, but I knew

C) it. I knew

D) it, I knew

5.

A) She was

B) Because she was

C) Although she was

D) She being

6.

A) tired, and he
B) tired, he
C) tired; he
D) tired. He

7.

A) early because
B) early, because
C) early, being that
D) early. Because

8.

A) dishes, I
B) dishes I
C) dishes, and I
D) dishes; I

9.

A) within, while
B) within, and while
C) within while
D) within; while

EXERCISE 4

Label each part with subject, verb, subordinating conjunction (if any), and clause type (or phrase). Cross out any always-wrong answer choices. Finally, choose the correct answer.

1. Because she was <u>thirsty. She</u> drank some soda.

A) NO CHANGE

B) thirsty; she

C) thirsty, she

D) thirsty, so she

2. The journey was difficult; all the way to Mexico.

A) NO CHANGE

B) difficult, and all

C) difficult, being all

D) difficult all

3. My mother always used to cook delicious meals, but I later found out that she just microwaved everything.

A) NO CHANGE

B) meals, however I later

C) meals. But I later

D) meals; but I later

4. Although he never said it; I knew my father was scared.

A) NO CHANGE

B) it, but I knew

C) it. I knew

D) it, I knew

5. She was thirsty, she drank water.

A) NO CHANGE

B) Because she was

C) Although she was

D) She being

6. Since the old man was <u>tired, and he</u> went to sleep early.

A) NO CHANGE
B) tired, he
C) tired; he
D) tired. He

7. The old man went to sleep <u>early because</u> he was tired.

A) NO CHANGE
B) early, because
C) early, being that
D) early. Because

8. While I washed <u>dishes, I</u> whistled a happy tune to quell the despair within.

A) NO CHANGE
B) dishes I
C) dishes, and I
D) dishes; I

9. I whistled a happy tune to quell the despair <u>within, while</u> I washed dishes.

A) NO CHANGE
B) within, and while
C) within while
D) within; while

CHAPTER 16 ANSWER KEY

EXERCISE 1

1.

    1. . (period)

    2. ; (semicolon)

    3. ,FANBOYS (comma FANBOYS)

2.

1. DEP , IND

2. IND DEP **(no comma)**

EXERCISE 2

1. C.

The strapping young fellow decided to try his luck

he shot the bullet at the target.

First part subject: **The strapping young fellow**

First part verb: **decided**

Second part subject: **he**

Second part verb: **shot**

Subordinating conjunction, if any: **(none)**

The first part is **IND clause**/not a complete clause. The second part is **IND clause**/not a complete clause.

2. D.

The frightened dog pondered his past

and decided never to return.

First part subject: **The frightened dog**

First part verb: **pondered**

Second part subject: **(none)**

Second part verb: **decided**

Subordinating conjunction, if any: **(none; "and" is a FANBOYS)**

The first part is **IND clause**/not a complete clause. The second part is
_____ clause/**not a complete clause (it is missing a subject)**.

3. A.

After I ate dinner

I considered watching a movie.

First part subject: **I**

First part verb: **ate**

Second part subject: **I**

Second part verb: **considered**

Subordinating conjunction, if any: **After**

The first part is **DEP clause**/not a complete clause. The second part is **IND clause**/not a complete clause.

4. B.

I was tired

I went to bed.

First part subject: **I**

First part verb: **was**

Second part subject: **I**

Second part verb: **went**

Subordinating conjunction, if any: **(none)**

The first part is **IND clause**/not a complete clause. The second part is **IND clause**/not a complete clause.

EXERCISE 3

1. Cross out A, B, and (probably) D. They are grammatically the same: a period is the same as a semicolon, which is grammatically the same as a comma FANBOYS.

2. Cross out C because "being" is always wrong. Cross out A and B because a semicolon is grammatically the same as a comma FANBOYS.

3. Cross out C and D because you can always cross out period FANBOYS and semicolon FANBOYS. Cross out B because "however" is always a non-essential comma phrase, so it must have a comma after it; in addition, "however" usually starts a new sentence.

4. Cross out A, B, and C. A period, semicolon, and comma FANBOYS are all grammatically the same.

5. Cross out D. "Being" is always wrong.

6. Cross out A, C, and D. Comma FANBOYS, semicolon, and period are grammatically the same.

7. Cross out C. "Being" is always wrong.

8. Cross out C and D. Comma FANBOYS and semicolon are grammatically the same.

9. Cross out B and D. Comma FANBOYS and semicolon are grammatically the same.

EXERCISE 4

1. C.

First part subject: she

First part verb: was

Subordinating conjunction: because

Second part subject: she

Second part verb: drank

The first part is **DEP clause**. The second part is **IND clause**.

2. D.

First part subject: the journey

First part verb: was

Subordinating conjunction: (none)

Second part subject: (none)

Second part verb: (none)

The first part is **IND clause**. The second part is **a phrase, not a clause**.

3. A.

First part subject: my mother

First part verb: used to cook

FANBOYS: but (using a comma FANBOYS to separate two independent clauses)

Second part subject: I

Second part verb: found out

The first part is **IND clause**. The second part is **IND clause**.

4. D.

First part subject: he

First part verb: said

Subordinating conjunction: although

Second part subject: I

Second part verb: knew

The first part is **DEP clause**. The second part is **IND clause**.

5. B.

First part subject: she

First part verb: was

(Subordinating conjunction: because)

Second part subject: she

Second part verb: drank

The first part is **DEP clause**. The second part is **IND clause**.

6. B.

First part subject: the old man

First part verb: was

Subordinating conjunction: since

Second part subject: he

Second part verb: went

The first part is **DEP clause**. The second part is **IND clause**.

7. A.

First part subject: the old man

First part verb: went

Subordinating conjunction: because

Second part subject: he

Second part verb: was

The first part is **IND clause**. The second part is **DEP clause**.

8. A.

First part subject: I

First part verb: washed

Subordinating conjunction: while

Second part subject: I

Second part verb: whistled

The first part is **DEP clause**. The second part is **IND clause**.

9. C.

First part subject: I

First part verb: whistled

Subordinating conjunction: while

Second part subject: I

Second part verb: washed

The first part is **IND clause**. The second part is **DEP clause**.

CLAUSE PUNCTUATION STUDY GUIDE!

Write 10 questions in your notebook for this study guide.

STUDY GUIDE ANSWER KEY

Write the answer key on the next page.

Chapter 17: Modifiers

"Modify" is grammar nerd-speak for "describe." Thus, modifiers are describers—any phrase that describes the word next to it. Here are some examples of modifiers:

Adjectives: The **big** dog

Prepositional phrases: The puppy **in the yard**

But the most important type of modifier appears at the beginning of a sentence, doesn't have a subject, has a comma at the end, and describes whatever comes after the comma.

Hot tip: If there is no subject, then the subject must be after the comma.

Here are some examples. The modifiers are **bolded**:

1. **Suddenly remembering the meeting,** she ran out of the room.

   (Who is remembering? **She** is, so "she" comes right after the comma.)

2. **Confused about what the teacher had said,** I raised my hand.

   (Who is confused? **I** am, so "I" comes right after the comma.)

3. **Chewing loudly,** my brother annoyed me.

   (Who is chewing? **my brother** is, so "my brother" comes right after the comma.)

Pattern alert!

Notice anything about the modifiers in sentences 1 and 3? They start, or nearly start, with an "ing" word.

Hot tip: If a sentence starts with an "ing" word, it is probably a modifier. Make sure the subject comes next.

Sentence 2 also has an important ending: "ed." Keep your eye out for "ed" words at the beginning of sentences, too; it's a pretty good sign that you're dealing with a modifier.

Fun fact: The formal grammatical name for an "ing" and "ed" modifier is a **participle**. You don't need to memorize that.

Misplaced Modifiers

Now, what's wrong with this sentence?

After eating all the dog food, I bid farewell to my dog and went to buy more.

First, notice the "ing" word near the beginning of the sentence. We are probably dealing with a modifier, so let's ask, "Who is eating all the dog food?" The subject should probably be "the dog," but the very next word after the comma is "I."

So, according to this sentence, who ate all the dog food?

I did.

Oops. Sorry, Sparky. Get your own kibble.

Let's fix the sentence by giving it the correct subject:

After eating all the dog food, **my dog** whined until I went to buy more.

Ah, that's better. Now, when we ask "who is eating all the dog food," the answer is "my dog."

But wait, there's more!

There's another way to add the correct subject, too. We could also put the subject in the first part, turning it into a dependent clause:

After **my dog** ate all the dog food, I bid farewell to him and went to buy more.

Hot tip: There are two ways to fix a misplaced modifier.

1. Put the correct subject after the comma

2. Put the correct subject near the beginning to change the modifier into a dependent clause

BRAIN DUMP!

Write down as much as you can remember from this chapter. DO THIS FROM MEMORY: DO NOT LOOK AT THE BOOK OR YOUR NOTES. You may want to set a timer for five or ten minutes and write continuously.

EXERCISE 1

Write the subject after the modifier. Fill in the blanks using **"I,"** **"the teacher,"** or **"the dog."** Ask "who/what is being modified?"

1. Tired after a long day of helping students, _____ went home.

2. After finishing my homework, _____ went outside.

3. Covered with beautiful brown fur, _____ was very cute.

4. Excited about graduating from high school, _____ texted all my friends.

5. Chasing the cat and barking, _____ was having a lot of fun.

6. Failing to truly understand the nature of atoms, _____ did not do very well on the chemistry quiz.

7. Having worked in the school for many years, _____ was well-known.

8. Studying hard for the test, _____ was surprised to look up and see it was 1 AM.

EXERCISE 2

Is there a misplaced modifier? Ask yourself who or what the modifier describes (its "subject"). Is that the next noun? If there is an error, rewrite the part **after** the modifier so that it has the correct subject.

(Hint: Only one of the below sentences has no error.)

The first one has been done for you.

1. Sleeping soundly all night, my alarm clock woke me up.

Rewrite: Sleeping soundly all night, **I woke up when I heard my alarm clock.**

2. Crispy and delicious, my mom finished frying the potatoes.

Rewrite: Crispy and delicious, _____.

3. After reading his most famous play, Shakespeare seemed more amazing than ever, in my opinion.

Rewrite: After reading his most famous play,

_____.

4. After I read his most famous play, Shakespeare seemed more amazing than ever.

Rewrite: After I read his most famous play,

_____.

5. Before sitting down to do my homework, my dog was taken for a walk.

Rewrite: Before sitting down to do my homework,

_____.

EXERCISE 3

Is there a modifier error? If so, fix it by using the other technique: change the modifier into a dependent clause by adding a subject.

The first one has been done for you.

1. Sleeping soundly all night, my alarm clock woke me up.

Rewrite: **Although I had been sleeping soundly all night,** my alarm clock woke me up.

2. Crispy and delicious, my mom finished frying the potatoes.

Rewrite: _____, my mom finished frying the potatoes.
3. After reading his most famous play, Shakespeare seemed more amazing than ever, in my opinion.

Rewrite: _____, Shakespeare seemed more amazing than ever, in my opinion.
4. After I read his most famous play, Shakespeare seemed more amazing than ever.

Rewrite: _____, Shakespeare seemed more amazing than ever.
5. Before sitting down to do my homework, my dog was taken for a walk.

Rewrite: _____, my dog was taken for a walk.

EXERCISE 4

Rewrite the sentences to correct the misplaced modifier; otherwise, write "NO ERROR":

1. Despite having stayed up all night to finish the project, the teacher still gave him a bad grade.

2. After staying awake for thirty hours straight, Sam's vision started to get blurry.

3. I found a box on my porch full of potatoes.

4. I was not sure what to expect when I first saw green ketchup, but after trying it, the flavor was not bad.

5. If I placed my chair just so, I could sit and watch the parade in my kitchen.

CHAPTER 17 ANSWER KEY

EXERCISE 1

1. the teacher

2. I

3. the dog

4. I

5. the dog

6. I

7. the teacher

8. I

EXERCISE 2 (answers may vary, but the **subject** must be as written)

1. Sleeping soundly all night, **I** woke up when I heard my alarm clock. (Who was sleeping soundly? **I** was, so **I** must be the subject after the comma.)

2. Crispy and delicious, **the potatoes** were finished.

3. After reading his most famous play, **I** thought Shakespeare was more amazing than ever.

4. **No error.** ("After I read" has a subject, so it is not a modifier. It is a dependent clause. Remember the punctuation rule: DEP , IND.)

5. Before sitting down to do my homework, **I** took my dog for a walk.

EXERCISE 3 (answers may vary, but the **subject** must be as written)

1. Although I had been sleeping soundly all night, my alarm clock woke me up. (Subject: **I**)

2. As **my mom** made sure they were crispy and delicious, my mom finished frying the potatoes.

3. After I read his most famous play, Shakespeare seemed more amazing than ever, in my opinion.

4. **No error.**

5. Before I sat down to do my homework, my dog was taken for a walk.

EXERCISE 4 (answers may vary, but the **subject** must be as written)

1. 1. Despite having stayed up all night to finish the project, he still got a bad grade. (Who stayed up? He did.)

2. 2. After staying awake for thirty hours straight, Sam couldn't see straight. (Who stayed awake? Sam did—Sam's vision didn't stay awake.)

3. 3. I found a box full of potatoes on my porch. (Prepositional phrases are modifiers, too, and must be next to what they describe.)

4. 4. I was not sure what to expect when I first saw green ketchup, but after trying it, I found that the flavor was not bad. (Who tried it? I did.)

5. 5. If I placed my chair just so, I could sit in my kitchen and watch the parade. (Prepositional phrases are modifiers, too, and must be next to what they describe. The parade was not in my kitchen.)

MODIFIERS STUDY GUIDE!

Write 10 questions in your notebook for this study guide.

STUDY GUIDE ANSWER KEY

Write the answer key on the next page.

Chapter 18: Colons

Give it a try: Figure out the colon rule!

Step 1. Label all independent or dependent clauses, remembering the difference between a clause and a phrase. (A clause has a subject and a verb.)

Step 2: Fill in the blanks to guess the colon rules.

Rule #1: A colon must have _____ before it.

1. CORRECT. I need to go to the store and buy a lot of things: milk, eggs, cheese, and burgers.

2. CORRECT. There are a lot of problems with this town: it's boring, the roads are unsafe, and the water tastes bad.

3. CORRECT. There are so many reasons why I love my friends: they're interesting, compassionate people, for one thing.

4. WRONG. I need to: go to the store, make dinner, and do my homework.

5. WRONG. I have a lot of: books, CDs, and DVDs.

6. WRONG. I need to go to the store and get: milk, eggs, cheese, and burgers.

Rule #2: A colon often has _____ after it, but not

always. Specifically, what comes after a colon is some kind of

_____.

Ready for the answers?

Rule #1: A colon must have **a full sentence** before it.

Rule #2: A colon often has **a list** after it, but not always. Specifically, what comes after a colon is some kind of **description of something before the colon**.

Rule #1 is by far the most important colon rule to remember for the test.

Hot tip: On the SAT/ACT, a colon must always have a full sentence before it.

In real life, we use colons for other things, but on the test, this rule is strict. Here are some examples of things you can always cross out because they violate Rule #1.

For example:

Such as:

Including:

Is "for example" a full sentence? No. Cross it out.

Is "such as" a full sentence? No. Cross it out.

Is "including" a full sentence? No. Cross it out.

Punctuating for example and such as

"For example" and "such as" appear so frequently on the test, they deserve their own section. Here is how to punctuate them, along with sample sentences:

For example,

Different people like different foods. **For example,** some people like sushi, while others prefer pizza.

The scientists found evidence to support their theory. **For example,** the bacteria population increased after one week.

, such as

> Different people like different foods, **such as** sushi or pizza.

> The scientists found evidence to support their theory, **such as** the increase in the bacteria population.

Note that "for example" usually starts a new sentence, but "such as" does not.

Hot tip: Memorize these punctuation rules:

For example,

, such as

Neither uses a colon.

BRAIN DUMP!

Write down as much as you can remember from this chapter. DO THIS FROM MEMORY: DO NOT LOOK AT THE BOOK OR YOUR NOTES. You may want to set a timer for five or ten minutes and write continuously.

EXERCISE 1

1. Colon Rule #1: _____

2. Colon Rule #2: _____

3. True/False: "For example" has a colon after it.

4. True/False: "Such as" has a colon after it.

EXERCISE 2

Cross out any always-wrong answer choices. You can cross out at least 2 answer choices in each question.

1.

    A) Such as:

    B) For example:

    C) Such as,

    D) For example,

2.

    A) said. For example:

    B) said; for example:

    C) said. For example,

    D) said for example

3.

    A) perspective such as,

    B) perspective. Such as:

    C) perspective; such as:

    D) perspective, such as

4.

    A) allowed for example

    B) allowed. For example:

    C) allowed; for example,

    D) allowed; for example:

CHAPTER 18 ANSWER KEY

EXERCISE 1

1. Colon Rule #1: A colon must have a full sentence before it.

2. Colon Rule #2: A colon often has a list after it, but not always. Specifically, what comes after a colon is some kind of description of something before the colon.

3. False.

4. False.

EXERCISE 2

1.

~~A) Such as:~~ ("Such as" is not a full sentence, and a colon must have a full sentence before it.)

~~B) For example:~~ ("For example" is not a full sentence, and a colon must have a full sentence before it.)

~~C) Such as,~~ ("Such as" has a comma before it, not after it.)

D) For example, (Hooray! D is the right answer.)

2.

~~A) said. For example:~~ ("For example" is not a full sentence, and a colon must have a full sentence before it.)

~~B) said; for example:~~ ("For example" is not a full sentence, and a colon must have a full sentence before it.)

C) said. For example, (Yay! C is the right answer.)

~~D) said for example~~ ("For example" requires a comma after it.)

3.

~~A) perspective such as,~~ ("Such as" requires a comma before it, not after.)

~~B) perspective. Such as:~~ ("Such as" is not a full sentence, and a colon must have a full sentence before it.)

~~C) perspective; such as:~~ ("Such as" is not a full sentence, and a colon must have a full sentence before it.)

D) perspective, such as (Yippee! D is the right answer.)

4.

    A) allowed for example (This isn't necessarily wrong, depending on the context, so we can't completely cross it out, but it is probably wrong.)

    ~~B) allowed. For example:~~ ("For example" is not a full sentence, and a colon must have a full sentence before it.)

    C) allowed; for example, (This is almost certainly the right answer. However, we should read the sentence carefully to make sure option A isn't correct.)

    ~~D) allowed; for example:~~ ("For example" is not a full sentence, and a colon must have a full sentence before it.)

COLONS STUDY GUIDE!

Write 10 questions in your notebook for this study guide.

STUDY GUIDE ANSWER KEY

Write the answer key on the next page.

Chapter 19: Apostrophes

Possession

Apostrophes show possession. That is, if a noun has an apostrophe, then it has the next word.

Here are some examples:

> Bob's car (Bob has a car)
>
> Shauna's curly hair (Shauna has curly hair)

You can also think of apostrophes as standing in for "of":

> Bob's car (= The car of Bob)
>
> Shauna's curly hair (= The curly hair of Shauna)

Thankfully, apostrophes on the SAT follow the same rules as apostrophes in English class, so you may already be familiar with them.

There are three main possessive apostrophe rules to learn. Try to figure them out!

FIGURE OUT THE APOSTROPHE RULE

Step 1: Underline the word that has an apostrophe.

Step 2: Circle the noun after it, which it "has."

Step 3: Guess the apostrophe rules! Fill in the blanks.

Rule #1: For _____ nouns, the apostrophe goes _____ the "s."

1. CORRECT. This is my friend's house. I love his mom's food.

2. CORRECT. My father's name is Arthur.

3. CORRECT. My family's favorite game is Monopoly.

4. CORRECT. The team's color is blue.

5. CORRECT. The business's name is Apple.

6. ~~WRONG. The business' name is Apple.~~

7. ~~WRONG. My sisters' name is Jessica.~~

8. WRONG. My best friends' goldfish died, and she was despondent.

Rule #2: For _____ nouns, the apostrophe goes _____

1. CORRECT. My friends' music taste is excellent, and that's why I admire them.

2. CORRECT. My dogs' barking is always loud, but I love them anyway.

3. WRONG. I am constantly embarrassed by my friend's outfits, because none of my friends have any fashion sense.

4. WRONG. Please come to my parent's house for dinner; they would love to meet you.

Rule #3: For _____ nouns that don't _____, the

apostrophe goes _____ (just like Rule # _____ for

_____ nouns).

1. CORRECT. The men's bathroom is over here.

2. CORRECT. Everyone loves to hear children's laughter.

3. WRONG. Where is the womens' room?

4. WRONG. The geeses' honking was really loud.

Ready for the answer?

Rule #1: For **singular** nouns, the apostrophe goes **before** the "s."

Rule #2: For **plural** nouns, the apostrophe goes **after the "s."**

Rule #3: For **plural** nouns that don't **end in "s,"** the

apostrophe goes **before the "s"** (just like Rule # **1** for

singular nouns).

Another way to think of it is this:

The full word—that is, the thing that is possessing—goes before the apostrophe. Here's what that means:

Singular nouns:

1. This is my **friend's** house. (The house of my **friend**, so the apostrophe goes after **friend** and before the "s.")

2. I love his **mom's** food. (The food of his **mom**, so the apostrophe goes after **mom** and before the "s.")

Plural nouns that end in "s":

3. All my **friends'** music taste is excellent, and that's why I admire them. (The music taste of all my **friends**, so the apostrophe goes after **friends**.)

4. My **dogs'** barking is always loud, but I love them anyway. (The barking of my **dogs**, so the apostrophe goes after **dogs**.)

Plural nouns that don't end in "s":

5. The **men's** bathroom is over here. (The bathroom of the **men**, so the apostrophe goes after **men** and before the "s.")

6. Everyone loves to hear **children's** laughter. (The laughter of **children**, so the apostrophe goes after **children** and before the "s.")

Pronouns & contractions

In addition to possession, apostrophes can be used to form contractions: combining two words into one. Here are some examples:

Do not → Don't

Is not → Isn't

Have not → Haven't

Whenever you see an apostrophe with a pronoun, it is a contraction.

Here are some of the most commonly confused pronoun contractions vs. possessives:

Possessive	Contraction
Its The fish ate **its** dinner.	It's (it is) **It's** hot out.
Their All the students did **their** homework.	They're (they are) I think **they're** hardworking.
Your Did you finish **your** homework?	You're (you are) **You're** very kind.
Whose **Whose** books are those?	Who's (who is) **Who's** going to the party?

Hot tip: Read "it's" as "it is" and "they're" as "they are."

Note: "There" can also be confusing. Remember the spelling this way:

Here and **there**.

BRAIN DUMP!

Write down as much as you can remember from this chapter. DO THIS FROM MEMORY: DO NOT LOOK AT THE BOOK OR YOUR NOTES. You may want to set a timer for five or ten minutes and write continuously.

EXERCISE 1

Fix the apostrophe errors. If there are no errors, write NO CHANGE.

1. This is my friend John's book.

2. The kid's all went out to play.

3. My friend's big dog is fluffy and awesome.

4. The girl's love playing sports.

5. I love pizza's delicious smell.

6. Where is the women's room?

7. Lizard's are really interesting creatures.

8. My mother's ideas' are the best.

9. My friend's sister's cat is adorable and cuddly.

10. My friend's brother's are very tall.

EXERCISE 2

Step 1: When you see "it's," "they're," or "you're," write out the full words: "it is," "they are," and "you are."

Step 2: Is the sentence correct or incorrect? If there is a mistake, fix it.

1. Its hot outside today.

2. The dog wagged its tail.

3. I don't think its cold enough to snow.

4. Their always late to class.

5. The guinea pigs ate their dinner.

6. They're always tired after a long day of studying.

7. They're is my book! I've been looking everywhere for it.

8. The students complained about there homework.

9. Where is your notebook?

10. Did you forgot you're homework again?

11. If you don't do your homework, you're in big trouble.

CHAPTER 19 ANSWER KEY

EXERCISE 1

1. No error.

2. The **kids** all went out to play.

3. No error.

4. The **girls** love playing sports.

5. No error.

6. No error.

7. **Lizards** are really interesting creatures.

8. My mother's **ideas** are the best.

9. No error.

10. My friend's **brothers** are very tall.

EXERCISE 2

1. **It's** hot outside today.

2. No error.

3. I don't think **it's** cold enough to snow.

4. **They're** always late to class.

5. No error.

6. No error.

7. **There** is my book! I've been looking everywhere for it.

8. The students complained about **their** homework.

9. No error.

10. Did you forget **your** homework again?

11. No error.

APOSTROPHES STUDY GUIDE!

Write 10 questions in your notebook for this study guide.

STUDY GUIDE ANSWER KEY

Write the answer key on the next page.

Chapter 20: Parallelism

Items in a list need to be in parallel. When you see a list, look for the other items on the list to decide whether they all match grammatically. Here are some examples of common parallelism errors and how to fix them.

Incorrect parallelism (bad)	Correct parallelism (good)
I like hiking, reading, and **to watch movies**. **What's wrong?** "Hiking" and "reading" don't include "to."	I like hiking, reading, and **watching movies**.
Next year, he plans to go to college, **to study hard**, and join a fraternity. **What's wrong?** "Join a fraternity" doesn't include "to."	Next year, he plans to go to college, **study hard**, and join a fraternity. (This is best because it is parallel **and** shorter is better.) **Or** Next year, he plans to go to college, to study hard, and **to join a fraternity.** (This is also parallel, so it is also correct, albeit a little longer.)
Our students must exhibit integrity, honesty, and **work hard**. **What's wrong?** "Integrity" and "honesty" are nouns, but "work" is a verb. We need another noun to match.	Our students must exhibit integrity, honesty, and **a hardworking attitude.**
I like ice cream, cake, and **eating cookies.** **What's wrong?** "Eating cookies" doesn't match—there are no other gerunds ("ing" words).	I like ice cream, cake, and cookies.
I enjoy playing music, going to concerts, and **books.** **What's wrong?** "Books" doesn't match "playing" and "going." We need another gerund ("ing" word).	I enjoy playing music, going to concerts, and **reading books.**

Comparisons

What's wrong with this sentence?

> X My hair is longer than my sister.

Well, it seems to be comparing hair to a sister; that is, it kind of sounds like I'm saying that my hair is longer than my sister is tall. That would be over five feet of hair and is definitely not what I wanted to say.

We need to compare hair to hair.

Let's fix it by being more specific. All three of these are grammatically correct ways to fix the sentence:

1. My hair is longer than my sister's hair.
2. My hair is longer than my sister's.
3. My hair is longer than that of my sister.

The SAT/ACT particularly likes to use the sentence 3 structure: "that of."

Here's another example of a bad sentence:

> X This year's profits are higher than last year.

It might sound OK initially, but this is comparing profits to last year, and we need to compare profits to profits. Here are three correct ways to fix it:

1. This year's profits are higher than last year's profits.
2. This year's profits are higher than last year's.
3. This year's profits are higher than those of last year.

Hot tip: If the sentence has a comparison, the correct answer will often include something like "that of" or "those of." When it comes to comparisons, shorter is **not** always better.

BRAIN DUMP!

Write down as much as you can remember from this chapter. DO THIS FROM MEMORY: DO NOT LOOK AT THE BOOK OR YOUR NOTES. You may want to set a timer for five or ten minutes and write continuously.

EXERCISE

1. When a bear came to town, the news was in the newspaper, on TV, <u>and the radio.</u>

    A) NO CHANGE

    B) the radio.

    C) and on the radio.

    D) as well as the radio.

2. The bear displayed <u>being enthusiastic</u> and curious personality.

    A) NO CHANGE

    B) an enthusiastic

    C) enthusiasm

    D) what was an enthusiastic

3. The bear wandered down the road, traipsed into yards, <u>and lumbered into the town square.</u>

    A) NO CHANGE

    B) into the town square

    C) and into the town square

    D) as well as into the town square

4. After he got tired of his urban exploration, the bear ate some snacks, turned back, <u>and had disappeared into the woods.</u>

    A) NO CHANGE

B) was disappearing into the woods.

C) and disappeared, having been going into the woods.

D) and disappeared into the woods.

5. Thanks to the bear, that week's newspaper was much more interesting than <u>the previous week.</u>

    A) NO CHANGE
    B) that of the previous week.
    C) the prior week.
    D) the week.

6. The content of that week's newspaper was more entertaining <u>than a novel.</u>

    A) NO CHANGE
    B) then a novel.
    C) than that of a novel.
    D) then those of a novel.

7. My sister's reaction, much like <u>that of my brother,</u> was one of amusement.

    A) NO CHANGE
    B) my brother,
    C) those of brother,
    D) of my brothers,

ANSWER KEY

1. C. "On the radio" is in parallel with "in the newspaper" and "on TV." They are all prepositional phrases.

2. B. "Enthusiastic" is in parallel with "curious." They are both adjectives. In addition, A is wrong because it uses "being," and D is too wordy.

3. A. "Lumbered into the town square" is in parallel with "wandered down the road" and "traipsed into yards." They all start with a verb and end with a prepositional phrase.

4. D. "Disappeared" is in parallel with "ate" and "turned." They are all simple past tense verbs.

5. B. We have to compare newspapers to newspapers, and A, C, and D all compare newspapers to weeks. In B, "that of" stands in for "the newspaper of."

6. C. We have to compare content to content; "that of a novel" in C stands in for "the content of a novel." B and D spell "then" instead of the comparative "than."

7. A. We need to compare reaction to reaction, and "that of my brother" stands in for "the reaction of my brother."

PARALLELISM STUDY GUIDE!

Write 10 questions in your notebook for this study guide.

STUDY GUIDE ANSWER KEY

Write the answer key on the next page.

Chapter 21. Transition Words

Transition words are those little non-essential adverbs like "however" and "moreover" that tell us the relationship between a sentence and the sentence **before** it. They come wrapped in a happy little burrito made of commas: that is, we say

> I, however, do not have a dog.

And we do not say

> I however do not have a dog.

Using transition words on the SAT/ACT is essentially the same as using transition words in real life, which means as long as you read carefully and pay close attention to the short list of tricky words, you should be in good shape.

Transition word technique

1. Get the main idea of the target sentence and the **previous** sentence.

2. Ask, "What is the relationship?"

Hot tip: Sometimes, the right answer is to delete the transition word or replace it with something not particularly meaningful. You can recognize this when you ask "What is the relationship?" and none of the answer choices represent that relationship.

Real-life application: Spice up your writing with transition words. Instead of the drab "firstly" and "secondly," use meaningful transition words to emphasize how your ideas interrelate.

The following chart includes the most common and trickiest transition words. I recommend memorizing it.

How does this sentence relate to the previous sentence?	Transition words
Opposite/contrasting.	However, on the other hand, while*
Opposite/contrasting. This sentence is unexpected. "Yes, but…"	Nevertheless, despite/in spite of, granted

Another fact. It's adding a new example to support a point.	Furthermore, moreover, in addition, not to mention*
Expanding upon the same fact. It's giving an example to support the previous sentence.	Indeed, in fact, for example, for instance, to illustrate
Cause and effect. The previous sentence caused this sentence.	Therefore, thus, consequently, accordingly
Summary. It paraphrases the main idea of the previous sentence without adding new information.	In conclusion, in short, in other words

"While" and "not to mention" are grammatically different and do not have a comma directly afterwards.

Let's try one together:

I have always loved reading books. <u>Indeed,</u> even as a child, I toted a book with me everywhere I went. Reading was my escape.

Before we look at the answer choices, let's do Steps 1 and 2:

1. Get the main idea of the target sentence and the **previous** sentence.

2. Ask, "What is the relationship?"

Let's paraphrase the target sentence (ignoring the underlined part): As a kid, I always carried a book around. And the previous sentence: I have loved reading forever.

Next, what is the relationship? Well, the target sentence illustrates an example of how I used to love reading, so it is giving a specific example to support the previous sentence. Which words from the chart show that relationship?

If you're not sure, I recommend studying it again. These are the words we're looking for: Indeed, in fact, for example, for instance, to illustrate.

Are any of these, or similar, words in the answer choices?

A) NO CHANGE

B) In the same way,

C) Moreover,

D) In conclusion,

The answer is **A**.

Notice that we did not even use the sentence after the target. This is because transition words relate the target sentence with the previous sentence.

Let's try one more:

New York is an amazing place to visit. It has incredible fine dining establishments. <u>In fact</u>, there are many hole-in-the-wall pizzerias with delicious $1 pizza slices.

Before we look at the answer choices, let's do Steps 1 and 2:

1. Get the main idea of the target sentence and the previous sentence.

2. Ask, "What is the relationship?"

Let's paraphrase the target sentence (ignoring the underlined part): There are great, cheap $1 pizzerias. And the previous sentence: New York has great fancy restaurants.

Next, what is the relationship? Well, the target sentence gives an example of a cheap restaurant that is good, and the previous sentence describes a different kind of restaurant that is expensive but is also good in a different way. The target sentence is giving a new example, different from the previous sentence, to support the overall point that New York is great to visit. This means we should use something along these lines: Furthermore, moreover, in addition, not to mention.

Are any of these, or similar, words in the answer choices?

A) NO CHANGE

B) However,

C) Moreover,

D) For example,

The answer is C.

BRAIN DUMP!

Write down as much as you can remember from this chapter. DO THIS FROM MEMORY: DO NOT LOOK AT THE BOOK OR YOUR NOTES. You may want to set a timer for five or ten minutes and write continuously.

EXERCISE 1

Fill in the blanks on this chart:

memorizing it.

How does this sentence relate to the previous sentence?	Transition words
Opposite/contrasting.	_____, on the other hand, _____
Opposite/contrasting. This sentence is unexpected. "Yes, but…"	_____, _____/in spite of, granted
Another fact. It's adding a new example to support a point.	_____, moreover, __ _____, not to mention
Expanding upon the same fact. It's giving an example to support the previous sentence.	_____, __ _____, for example, for instance, __ _____
Cause and effect. The previous sentence caused this sentence.	Therefore, _____, consequently, accordingly
Summary. It paraphrases the main idea of the previous sentence without adding new information.	__ _____, in short, in other words

EXERCISE 2

1. It is a nice day. <u>Consequently</u>, I am staying inside.

   A) NO CHANGE

   B) Indeed,

   C) By the same token,

   D) However,

2. Scott likes to forage for mushrooms to add to his pasta. <u>In addition</u>, Sam goes fishing in his free time, hoping to catch something for dinner.

   A) NO CHANGE

   B) Similarly,

   C) Consequently,

   D) Furthermore,

3. Rebecca called up her friends to invite them to a picnic. <u>Next</u>, four people were able to attend.

   A) NO CHANGE

   B) Granted,

   C) In the end,

   D) In conclusion,

4. Few of the town's inhabitants considered television to be a major influence in their lives. <u>In fact</u>, fewer than half of the households reported owning a television set.

   A) NO CHANGE

   B) Furthermore,

   C) Nonetheless,

   D) However,

EXERCISE 3

1. No matter how much the children pleaded, the parents refused to buy them the latest technology. <u>In fact</u>, nobody in the family had a smartphone until college.

    A) NO CHANGE

    B) Not to mention

    C) Furthermore,

    D) Finally,

2. Alex studied harder for that test than he ever had in his life. <u>Ultimately</u>, he ended up spending over 50 hours reviewing his notes and quizzing himself in the end.

    A) NO CHANGE

    B) Indeed,

    C) Furthermore,

    D) Therefore,

3. I always found the idea of pineapple on pizza revolting. <u>Thus</u>, when I actually tried it, I enjoyed the burst of fruity flavor.

    A) NO CHANGE

    B) For instance,

    C) In particular,

    D) However,

4. There are many factors that contribute to lifelong health. Regular exercise is a key to longevity. <u>Furthermore</u>, eating a low-sugar diet may contribute to a long life.

    A) NO CHANGE

    B) For example,

    C) Indeed,

    D) However,

CHAPTER 21 ANSWER KEY

EXERCISE 1

See the chart earlier in the chapter.

EXERCISE 2

1. D. The target sentence, "I am staying inside" contrasts with what would be expected when it is a nice day.

2. B. The sentences give two distinct examples of different people looking for food outside in different ways. C indicates cause and effect, which is not accurate. A and D are not accurate because the sentences are not supporting any particular point; rather, they are comparing two similar activities.

3. C. The relationship here does not fit neatly into our chart, which suggests that the words from the chart may not be appropriate. This is simply a relationship where the sentences follow in a logical order. However, option A is not appropriate because "next" implies that there is a list of procedures.

4. A. The target sentence provides a specific detail that supports the previous sentence. Option B is wrong because the target sentence offers supporting evidence of the previous sentence; it is not a new and different fact.

EXERCISE 3

1. A. The target sentence provides a specific example that expands upon the previous sentence. Not having a smartphone until college describes a type of technology that the parents did not buy. B and C are wrong because they imply that these are two completely separate facts.

2. B. The target sentence paints a detailed picture of the previous sentence. Spending 50 hours reviewing and quizzing elaborates on how Alex studied. A is incorrect because it is redundant: the sentence ends with "in the end," which means the same thing as "ultimately."

3. D. The sentences are opposites. The target sentence says I enjoyed it, but the previous sentence says I found the idea disgusting.

4. A. The target and previous sentences are two separate examples of different factors that relate to lifelong health. B and C are wrong because they would imply that the target sentence is an example of the previous sentence, but a low-sugar diet is not an example of exercise. They are two separate facts.

TRANSITION WORD STUDY GUIDE!

Write 10 questions in your notebook for this study guide.

STUDY GUIDE ANSWER KEY

Write the answer key on the next page.

Chapter 22. Word Choice

Word choice means exactly what it sounds like. Which word sounds better? Consider connotation and tone. Is the word positive or negative? Where have you heard that word before? Here's an example:

>   The modern artist was famous for his <u>unique</u> paintings.

A) NO CHANGE

B) abnormal

C) weird

D) exorbitantly peculiar

Notice that all the answer choices mean essentially the same thing. This is common for word choice questions.

Think about connotation and where you have heard the words before. The connotation of "unique" is mostly positive. You may have heard someone say, "That jacket is so unique; I want it!" "Abnormal" is negative and has an almost medical connotation. You may have heard the doctor on a medical TV show say, "The scan shows an abnormal growth." "Weird" is negative and is overly casual; you wouldn't read it in a formal essay. "Exorbitantly peculiar" falls on the other end of the spectrum: it's way too highfalutin and formal. The Writing test avoids overly fancy language.

Which connotation do you want? Well, the artist was famous for the paintings, so we probably want a positive word. Read the sentence and fill in your own answer from whatever word pops into your head. I would probably say "The modern artist was famous for his distinct paintings," or even use the word "unique" myself. A is the answer.

To recap, for word choice questions:

1. Ask what connotation is needed. Read the sentence and fill in the blank with the first word that comes to mind.

2. Cross out any answer choices that are too casual or too fancy.

3. Choose the answer choice that fits the context.

Commonly confused words

While spelling is hardly a major component of the SAT/ACT, there are a number of commonly confused words that they may test you on. You should know when to use each of these words:

allusion/illusion

allude/elude

compliment/complement

except/accept

its/it's

respectfully/respectively

stationary/stationery

then/than

These are some of the most important commonly confused words to know. If this is an area in which you struggle, you can find free lists of commonly confused words and their definitions on online flashcard sites or books.

BRAIN DUMP!

Write down as much as you can remember from this chapter. DO THIS FROM MEMORY: DO NOT LOOK AT THE BOOK OR YOUR NOTES. You may want to set a timer for five or ten minutes and write continuously.

EXERCISE 1

1. When you stare at the image, the lines appear to move, <u>creating an optical allusion</u>.

   A) NO CHANGE

   B) forming an optical illusion

   C) a cool example of a trick

   D) being illusive optics

2. The toddler refused to eat anything <u>accept</u> mashed potatoes.

   A) NO CHANGE

   B) with the exception of

   C) except

   D) accepting

3. While some argue that <u>science is more important then the humanities</u>, many disagree with such a sweeping generalization.

   A) NO CHANGE

   B) the sciences have a greater importance then the humanities

   C) there is a greater import to science than there is to the humanities

   D) science is more important than the humanities

4. The attorney <u>respectfully disagreed</u>.

   A) NO CHANGE

   B) respectively disagreed

   C) showed disagreement with respect

   D) was really mad.

CHAPTER 22 ANSWER KEY

EXERCISE 1

1. B. The spelling needed here is "optical illusion." A is wrong because it uses "allusion," which means "indirectly referencing something." C is too casual. D is wrong because "being" is (almost) never correct on the Writing test; in addition, "optical illusion" is the correct idiom.

2. C. The spelling needed here is "except." A and D are wrong because "accept" means to receive (i.e. "I accepted the gift"). B is too wordy and redundant.

3. D. Although the answer choices appear to vary in many ways, the most important way is "then" vs. "than." When comparing things (greater than, less than, bigger than, smaller than, etc.), we must use "than." Thus, we can cross out A and B. C is too wordy; shorter is better.

4. A. B is wrong because "respectively" means "in order;" it has nothing to do with acting with respect. C is too wordy; A says the same thing more concisely, so shorter is better. D is too casual ("really" and "mad" are too colloquial for the SAT/ACT.)

WORD CHOICE STUDY GUIDE!

Write 10 questions in your notebook for this study guide.

STUDY GUIDE ANSWER KEY

Write the answer key on the next page.

INTERLEAVING PRACTICE TEST 2

This test includes all grammar question types.

Should you take the SAT/ACT?

Applying to college is hard enough. Do you really need (1) to take a standardized test like the (2) SAT; too? Unfortunately, the answer 99% of the time is "yes." Some colleges, including more than one top-ranked (3) universities, do not require the SAT or ACT, but many do. If you are certain that the schools to which you are applying do not require or recommend (4) the SAT—which you can find out by checking the website or emailing an admissions officer—and that there are no (5) relevant scholarship's that require it, then by all means, skip the test.

However, although nobody (6) expects to change their mind, just in case, it is a good idea to take the SAT or ACT. After you take the (7) PSAT: you will most likely be inundated with mail from colleges all over the country, some of which may offer you significant scholarships and even full rides. Imagine getting a letter from a college offering you a chance at a full scholarship—and (8) finding yourself ineligible to apply because you didn't take the SAT/ACT! (9) Granted, in this hypothetical case, you could call the admissions office and (10) explaining your situation. Still, (11) why take, the risk?

1. A) NO CHANGE
   B) to be taking
   C) take
   D) to be doing

2. A) NO CHANGE

   B) SAT, and too?

   C) SAT: too?

   D) SAT, too?

3. A) NO CHANGE

   B) universities, does

   C) university, do

   D) university, does

4. A) NO CHANGE

   B) the SAT, which

   C) the SAT which

   D) the SAT;

5. A) NO CHANGE

   B) relevant scholarships

   C) relevant scholarships'

   D) relevant scholarships's

6. A) NO CHANGE

   B) expect to change their mind

   C) expects to change his or her mind

   D) expects to change one's mind

7. A) NO CHANGE

   B) PSAT; you

C) PSAT, so you

D) PSAT, you

8. A) NO CHANGE

    B) find

    C) to find

    D) found

9. A) NO CHANGE

    B) Granted in

    C) Granted. In

    D) Granted: in

10. A) NO CHANGE

    B) explained

    C) having explained

    D) explain

11. A) NO CHANGE

    B) why take the

    C) why, take the

    D) why take

1. A. This uses the standard "need + infinitive verb" construction; that is, "need to" goes together. We can cross out C because it is missing "to." We can cross out B and D because they are needlessly wordy. A is best because it is the shortest, simplest option that isn't missing something important. **Review the Verbs chapter.**

2. D. "Too" is a non-essential comma phrase. We can cross out A and B because a semicolon and comma FANBOYS are grammatically the same. C is wrong because although there is a full sentence before the colon (Rule 1), what comes next ("too") does not elaborate upon any word before the colon (Rule 2). **Review the Colons chapter.**

3. C. Two things are changing in the answer choices: university/universities and do/does. First, let's figure out the subject of "do/does." Reading the sentence as a whole, we can cross out the non-essential "including more than one top-ranked university," revealing the plural subject: "some colleges." Since the subject is plural, we can cross out any options that use the singular "does." We are left with only A and C. Next, should we say "more than one university" or "more than one universities?" Because of "one," we use the singular. **Review the chapters on Verbs, Nouns, and Pronouns.**

4. A. This dash, in addition to the dash after "officer," offset this as a nonessential. **Review the Dashes chapter.**

5. B. No apostrophe is needed because there is no possession: "Scholarships" don't possess the next word. **Review the Apostrophes chapter.**

6. C. "Nobody" is singular, so it requires a singular verb ("expects") and a singular pronoun ("his or her"). **Review the Indefinite Pronouns chapter.**

7. D. "After you take the PSAT" is a dependent clause (subject: you; verb: take; subordinating conjunction: after). Options A, B, and C require two independent clauses. **Review the Clause Punctuation chapter.**

8. A. "Finding" is in parallel with "getting" earlier in the sentence. **Review the Parallelism chapter.**

9. A. "Granted" is a non-essential transition word, so it needs to be inside a comma phrase. We can also cross out C and D because "Granted" is not an independent clause. **Review these chapters: Crossing Out Comma Phrases and Clause Punctuation Rules.**

10. D. "Explain" is in parallel with "call" earlier in the sentence. **Review the Parallelism chapter.**

11. B. There is no reason to add a comma, so we can cross out A and C. D is missing the article "the." **Review the Clause Punctuation Rules chapter.**

Congratulations!

You did it! You finished the whole book!

Thank you for letting me guide you on your journey. If you have a minute, please leave an honest review on Amazon. Every little bit helps!

I often lead virtual programs about preparing for college, including SAT prep, ACT prep, college admissions essay workshops, study skills, and more. Want to hear about upcoming workshops or learn about tutoring options? Contact me at www.mindthetest.com.

Does your school or organization want quality college prep programming, including workshops, summer boot camps, and tutoring? Please email anna@mindthetest.com to discuss how we can work together.

About the Author

Anna is the founder of Mind the Test LLC, a New Jersey-based tutoring company empowering teens through brain-based study skills. The coolest fact about her is that she can read Egyptian hieroglyphs.

After earning a BA in Linguistics from the University of Chicago and a certification in Teaching English as a Foreign Language, she taught English and test preparation all around the world, spending summers as a cognitive psychology teaching assistant at the Johns Hopkins University Center for Talented Youth. She followed her passion for the science of learning to the University of Cambridge, where her MPhil thesis focused on improving educational equity via a grammatical analysis of the SAT.

When not teaching, Anna can be found reading about sociolinguistics, baking, and traveling.

Made in the USA
Monee, IL
08 July 2023

38859817R00090